Dharma – Its True Nature

An International Seminar

6-7 May 1995

Dhamma Giri, Igatpuri

Vipassana Research Institute

Dhamma Giri, Igatpuri 422 403

Dharma – Its True Nature

First Edition : 1995
Reprint : 2003, 2008, 2013, Dec. 2015

E12

ISBN 978-81-7414-124-8

Published by:
Vipassana Research Institute
Dhamma Giri, Igatpuri 422 403,
Dist. Nashik, Maharashtra, India Tel:
[91] (2553) 244998, 244076,
244086, 244144, 244440
Email: vri_admin@vridhamma.org
Website : www.vridhamma.org

Dharma – Its True Nature

Contents

		Page
Introduction		1
Opening Talk	Mr S.N. Goenka	4
Dharma—Its Definition and Universal Application	Mr S.N. Tandon	9
Discussion Extracts		21
Dharma—Its Role in Current Social Problems	Mrs Sally McDonald	26
Discussion Extracts		31
Dharma and Science	Professor P.L. Dhar	37
Discussion Extracts		47
Vipassana—a Practical Solution	Mr Ian Hetherington	48
Discussion Extracts		52
Seminar Overview	Mr N. Vaghul	57
Excerpts from Closing Talk	Mr S.N. Goenka	61
Dharma and Sectarianism	A Public Talk by S. N. Goenka	67
Vipassana Meditation Centres		**81**

Introduction

Background

The history of the evolution of civilisation is an incessant quest for social order based on justice, equality, peace, harmony and happiness. Men of wisdom in every country of the east, west, north and south have engaged in this quest.

India's contribution has been significant. It gave to the world a concept of Dhamma/Dharma, which embodies all the essentials of an ideal social order and is universally applicable without any distinction based on sex, caste, creed, sect, religion or nationality. It ensures freedom to the individual to shape his destiny in a manner of his own choosing, which is conducive to his personal development and happiness, and that of society as a whole, in the fields material as well as spiritual.

The Vipassana Research Institute is engaged in the scientific research on the theory and practice of Vipassana meditation: a technique of exploration and observation of mind-body phenomena leading to the purification of mind. The technique can bring about a major change in the attitude and behavioral pattern of the individual. The technique has a unique potential as an instrument to bring about change and improvement in the fields of Education, Health, Management in Government and Business, and Social Systems—strengthening the concept of secularism, national integration and international understanding.

The Institute has been organising annual seminars, national and international, dealing with various aspects of the above areas. In April 1994, the international seminar, organised at New Delhi, dealt with the subject "Vipassana Meditation—its Relevance to the Modern World".

This 1995 seminar was an outcome of the April 1994 event. The Institute feels that the Indian society, or for that matter the world society, is today at a crossroads in history. It is overwhelmed by the growth and advancement of science and technology—computers, genetics, electronics, media—on one side and on the other, gradual and sustained erosion of human values in all spheres of life. Communal, religious, ethnic, and caste conflicts, so rampant today, are stark manifestations of this reality.

Wisdom lies in understanding this phenomenon and taking corrective measures. This is part of man's eternal quest and in consonance with the great heritage of India. Accordingly the Institute selected the theme "Dharma—Its True Nature" for the 1995 seminar.

The objective of the seminar was very limited, yet very specific. The Institute had no wish to get involved in any controversy related to philosophical speculations and ideological differences and standpoints. The goal was to have a free and objective deliberation on different aspects of this important theme. A principal outcome would be a statement to create awareness of the problems and possible solutions and suggest an action plan to redeem society from this all-pervasive evil of ignorance of the essence of Dhamma.

International Seminar

The seminar was held at the Vipassana Research Institute, Igatpuri over the weekend of 6–7 May 1995. It was attended by leading persons from India and abroad. The 500 attendees came from diverse fields, such as cricketer Mr Bishen Bedi, educationist Mr Anil Bordia, and many prominent people in science, business, social work and politics, too numerous to mention. About forty foreign guests were present, from Europe, USA, Australia, Iran and neighbouring Asian countries.

The seminar was introduced by Shri S.N. Goenka, well-known and respected teacher of Vipassana meditation, who emphasized that Dharma is universal. He said pure dharma is not sectarian; we should not speak of Hindu dharma or Jain dharma, or Muslim or Christian dharma, but universal Dharma. It is a pure, harmonious and wholesome way of life, a life of morality.

The first working session included a scholarly talk on The Definition of Dharma by S.N. Tandon, who compared life to a game of snakes and ladders. When we are bitten by the snakes of our mental impurities or "unwholesome dharmas", we are dragged down to the snake pit, and when we develop good mental qualities, we climb a ladder towards enlightenment.

The second session covered The Role of Dharma in Current Social Problems. An international perspective was given by Mrs Sally McDonald from Australia, who discussed the stressful effects of modern life: population pressures, complex technology, mass media advertising and rapid rates of change. The role of Dharma, when defined as a path of self-introspection, is to eliminate the mental defilements that cause us to do wrong, to help us bear the stress of modern life, and to give us strength to serve and improve society.

Mr Bedi gave an entertaining talk on the "Dharma of Cricket" i.e., fair play, and more serious dissertations on economic and political aspects were given by speakers such as Mr Vidyadhar Gokhale and Mr Mohan Patel, ex-Sheriff of Bombay.

On Sunday morning a very stimulating talk on the complementary aspects of Dharma and Science was presented by Prof. P.L. Dhar of the Indian Institute of Technology, Delhi. He suggested that the ancient wisdom of Dharma, the fundamental insights of impermanence and constant change, were consistent with the emerging New World View of particle physics and molecular biology. He said both science and Dharma enunciate the laws of nature, and an understanding of both is needed to channel the power of modern developments for the very survival of humanity.

This was followed by a brief explanation of Vipassana meditation as a practical solution to so many of our personal and social problems, by Mr Ian Hetherington from the UK and Mr Ram Singh. Courses in Vipassana are attended by about 35,000 people worldwide each year. The technique involves the practice of morality, control over the mind, and a gradual but total purification of mind by examining one's own true nature.

The concluding session, led by eminent financier Mr N. Vaghul, drew up an action plan to incorporate the principles and teachings of pure Dharma into school education (11,000 schoolchildren are already attending introductory meditation courses each year) and into business corporations, government, etc. It was proposed that this will enhance the productivity and prosperity of nations at the same time as developing a sound ethical base for our society.

The closing address of the seminar was given by Mr S.N. Goenka. He welcomed the conclusion that practical steps are necessary to alleviate the miseries in modern society. For this we have to look to changing the mind of Man, a massive task. However, modest beginnings have already been made, and there is a precedent for what Vipassana can achieve on a mass scale in Emperor Aśoka's inspiring reign. To understand what Dharma is and the true meaning of the Buddha's words, it is essential to practise Vipassana and apply it in daily life. The technique provides a universal way out of suffering and is completely non-sectarian. He urged all participants at the seminar to move beyond discussion and taste the benefits of Dharma for themselves.

Opening Talk

S.N. Goenka

Reverend Monks and Dhamma friends:

We have all assembled here for these two days to understand what Dhamma, or Dharma, is and how to apply it in life.

A Life of Dharma

Dharma is a healthy, harmonious, wholesome way of life. It is a life of morality, of ethics. Dharma is an art of living: how to live peacefully and harmoniously within, and how to generate peace and harmony in the surrounding atmosphere, so that others can also live in peace and harmony. It is a way of life in which one does not perform any action, physical or vocal, to harm or hurt other beings.

One abstains from killing because by killing one harms others and disturbs the peace of society. One abstains from stealing. One abstains from sexual misconduct. One abstains from lying, from using harsh words, from backbiting or slander, and from useless or meaningless talk that wastes one's own time and the time of others. To abstain from all these improper, immoral activities, one also has to abstain from taking intoxicants. Once you start taking intoxicants, you become a slave to them. In a state of intoxication you keep on performing unwholesome actions in spite of understanding fully well at the intellectual level that you should not do so. Therefore one should abstain from all intoxicants.

At the apparent level, by living such a moral life without harming anybody, you are creating peace and harmony in society. Accordingly, you might feel that you are acting in this way to oblige others. But this is not correct. The fact is that when you abstain from performing unwholesome physical and vocal actions, you benefit yourself.

Dharma will help you understand why and how this is so, because Dharma is the universal law of nature applicable to everyone. You can understand this law not by attending seminars such as this, or by playing intellectual games, or by accepting something at the devotional or emotional level, but by realising the truth within yourself.

Harming Others, You Harm Yourself

Once you start investigating the truth within yourself, the law of nature will be revealed. Because of your intellectual understanding or because of your devotion to the teaching of the Enlightened One, you may remind yourself that you should not harm others. But when you go deep inside, you understand by experience that when you abstain from harming others, you actually abstain from harming yourself.

You cannot hurt or harm anyone unless you have first harmed yourself. You cannot kill anyone unless you have first killed the peace and harmony within you. You cannot kill anybody without generating a tremendous amount of anger, hatred, ill will, and animosity. When you generate such negativity you are the first victim because you become so miserable.

You cannot really understand this until you start observing the interaction of mind and matter within yourself, within the framework of this body. When you generate any negativity in the mind, it influences the body (matter), and there is bound to be an unpleasant physical sensation. That unpleasant sensation will again influence the negativity in your mind. When you generate more negativity, there will be more unpleasant sensations in the body; and with more unpleasant sensation in the body, there will be more negativity. A vicious circle starts of which you are a victim, and the result is great misery.

As the Buddha said, *Pubbe hanati attānaṃ, pacchā hanati so pare* [before killing another, one kills oneself].

Do not accept these words because they have been said by an enlightened person, or by your teacher; this will not help you at all. When you start realising the truth of the interaction of mind and matter inside yourself, it will become so clear. You will recognise that you have started harming yourself before harming someone else. And no-one wishes to do that.

If unintentionally you place your hand in a burning fire, it hurts you. After repeating the same mistake a few times, you will stop doing it because you know it hurts.

In the same way, if you start experiencing the truth inside—the truth which is to be accepted not merely intellectually or emotionally or devotionally, but at the actual level—you realise that you become miserable when you generate anger, passion, or egotism. If you keep realising this repeatedly, you will start abstaining from that type of action because you know it is not good for you.

We do not want to harm ourselves, but we keep doing so out of ignorance because we do not know the truth within. The truth outside is an apparent truth; it is only one dimension of the truth. You may think that you are unhappy because of things outside—because of other people who are behaving wrongly, or because of an unpleasant external situation. This is all apparent truth—in other words, truth seen from only one angle or in only one dimension. It is not the whole truth, but only a partial truth—and partial truth is a distorted truth, far away from the actual truth. When you see the truth from different angles, you start understanding the totality of the truth. And when you do, every decision you make will be a healthy decision; it will be good for you and for others.

What Happens at the Actual Level

If somebody has abused, insulted or misbehaved towards you, you become miserable. You may think you are miserable because of the abuse, insults or misbehaviour of that other person. At the apparent level this is true, but not at the deepest level.

We can understand this if we start realising the truth of the interaction of mind and matter, the influence of one over the other—if we divide, dissect, disintegrate, dissolve, like scientists or research scholars. As we do so, we shall see a process happening inside. Someone has spoken abuse; certain words have reached the ears; and immediately one part of the mind will simply cognise the sound.

Next a second part of the mind recognises the sound on the basis of memory and past experience: “Words. What words? Oh, words of abuse.” This same part of the mind then gives a valuation: “Words of abuse—that is very bad.”

Then the third part of the mind starts working—the part that feels sensations or vibrations. Sound is mere vibration, and as soon as the abusive words reached the ear they created vibrations throughout the body. However, the entire physical and mental structure itself is simply a mass of vibrations.

As the Buddha said, *Sabbo pajjalito loko, sabbo loko pakampito, pakampito* [the entire universe is nothing but combustion and vibration].

The words that came are nothing but vibration. And when they contact the mental-physical structure, which is a mass of vibration, a new vibration starts.

It is as if you strike a gong at a particular point and the entire gong starts vibrating. If a sound comes into contact with the ear, the entire structure of body and mind starts vibrating with a neutral vibration. When the second part of the mind gives its valuation saying "This is abuse—it is bad", immediately the originally neutral vibration becomes very unpleasant. And the feeling part of the mind feels that unpleasant sensation.

Then immediately, the fourth part of the mind starts working, and its job is to react: "Very unpleasant. I don't like it. Stop it. I don't like it." It has reacted with aversion and hatred.

Every time you generate aversion, hatred, ill will or animosity, you are miserable. You lose the balance of your mind; you lose the peace of your mind.

Dharma is Universal

This is the law. This is the truth. This is Dharma. It is not Buddhist, Hindu, Jain, Muslim, Christian, Parsi, or Sikh dharma. It is simply Dharma.

The moment you make it the exclusive property of a particular sect, Dharma is no longer Dharma. It has become sectarian and is harmful. You must understand that Dharma is universal. Dharma cannot be Buddhist, Hindu, Muslim or Christian. It is the law of nature.

For example, we say that the nature of fire is to burn. This is the dharma of fire. If it does not burn, it can't be fire. If it is fire it must burn.

When fire burns, do you label the burning as Hindu, Muslim, Buddhist or Jain burning, or as Indian, European, American or Russian burning? Burning is burning. This is a law of nature.

In the same way, when one generates any negativity or defilement in the mind, one is bound to burn. The nature of defilement is to burn. No-one can save you from burning when you generate anger. You may keep on calling yourself a Hindu, Buddhist, Christian, Muslim, Jain or Sikh—it makes no difference; or a *brāhmin* or a *śūdra*—it makes no difference. This is the law; this is nature; this is Dharma.

We have forgotten Dharma. Someone belongs to a certain sect and performs its rites or rituals, or professes its beliefs; he feels that makes him very Dharmic. Someone else belongs to another sect and performs its rites, rituals and ceremonies, or believes in its philosophy. He too thinks that makes him a very Dharmic person. But both deceive themselves.

Dharma has nothing to do with such matters. They are sectarian, and Dharma is universal. Whether or not we perform this rite or that ritual, if we keep the mind free of negativities it is pure. And according to the law of nature, when the mind is free from defilements it naturally fills with *mettā* (love), *karuṇā* (compassion), *muditā* (sympathetic joy), and *upekkhā* (equanimity); and immediately one starts enjoying peace and harmony.

Rites and rituals, philosophies and dogmas have nothing to do with it. We have forgotten the truth of Dharma deep inside—this universal law of nature makes no discrimination. Anyone who places a hand in burning fire is bound to burn oneself.

It makes no difference what religion one belongs to, what rites or rituals one performs, or what philosophy one believes in.

Experience Dharma

How can we understand this law? By listening to these discourses, we may intellectualise Dharma saying that this appears logical, rational and scientific. We may say that it should be applied in life, that we should not generate negativity because if we do we are bound to become miserable.

But the wisdom of mere Dharma assemblies dissipates the moment you leave. If these assemblies worked, India would be the most Dharmic country in the world; instead it is the biggest victim of sectarianism. No-one is interested in understanding Dharma at the experiential level, in realising it. Unless you do so, all these sermons are not going to help.

I know from my own experience that they did not help me. I was born in a family full of so-called Dharmic atmosphere, but nobody understood real Dharma. We knew no way to realise Dharma within.

Fortunately I had a second birth. The first was my physical emergence from the womb of my mother. But the second was my emergence from the shell of ignorance, thanks to my teacher, Sayagyi U Ba Khin. With his guidance I started experiencing the truth inside.

Dharma Works Here and Now

When you generate any impurity in the mind, you are punished at once. If you break the law of a country or state, you might manage to escape punishment or delay it for years.

But under the law of nature you cannot avoid the punishment or postpone it. Nature does not wait till you die. When you break the law you are punished that very moment. When you generate negativity in the mind, nature starts punishing you without delay.

If you do not break the law, if you live according to the law of nature and keep your mind pure, if you generate compassion and goodwill, then nature rewards you here and now. It will not wait until you die. You start experiencing peace and harmony here and now.

When one starts realising this law of nature at the experiential level, one starts taking steps on the path of Dharma; one starts attaining Dharma, experiencing Dharma, and receiving the best, sweetest fruits of Dharma in this very life.

But first one has to liberate Dharma from the shackles and chains of different sects. Every sect will take you far away from Dharma. When you start realising the truth of Dharma, you cannot remain sectarian. You cannot differentiate between this or that person, this or that being. The law is applicable everywhere, to everyone.

If I am really a Dharmic person, when somebody abuses me I understand that this is a miserable, sick person: "This person has generated anger and hatred, and is therefore very miserable. What should I generate in return? I cannot throw more petrol on this person who is burning in the fire of anger and hatred; instead I will generate love, compassion, goodwill. This is a sick person; why should I allow myself to succumb to the same sickness? Why generate anger towards this person?"

This is easy to understand and accept at the intellectual level; but at the real level, when someone abuses you, you start abusing that person in retaliation. This happens when you try to understand Dharma only intellectually rather than experientially.

Dharma is for All

Vipassana is not limited to a particular sect, community or caste. The law of nature is for everybody; and one starts realising this law by experiencing what happens inside.

Just as you have hospitals and schools, you also have meditation centres like this one, where people start realising and experiencing the truth of the law within themselves. They start living a better life, a proper life without harming others—which also means without harming themselves; and so they enjoy peace and harmony.

They also diffuse these pure vibrations into the surrounding atmosphere, and whoever comes into contact with them lives a life of peace and harmony as well. This is Dharma.

Recommendations

I would very much like those of you who have taken courses in Dharma to explore the truth inside at a deeper level. You have started scratching the reality inside only at the surface. The deeper you go, the more you will understand reality at the very subtle level, and the more your mind will be purified. Naturally, a time will come when it always remains pure, full of love and compassion. That cannot happen unless you go deep inside and start the process of purification. And you must do this yourself.

Accordingly I would recommend to those who have taken such courses that they go much deeper. A ten-day course is simply a beginning, to acquire an outline of what Dharma is. You have to take courses of twenty days, one month, one and a half months, and maybe later on of three months, so that you can really understand Dharma. Advance to the university level; don't remain in the kindergarten.

And those who have not yet entered the kindergarten, I would request them to do so and see what the truth is—the truth of the saints, sages, wise people, enlightened ones of this country.

Do not make Dharma a merely intellectual, emotional or devotional entertainment. Let it be an actual experience, for your own good, benefit, peace and harmony.

I am recommending this because I have passed through a life without Dharma, and yet felt myself to be a very Dharmic person. I gave thousands or tens of thousands in donations; and I would proudly say that, because I was a very generous donor, or I was the president of one or another temple, I must really be a Dharmic person. But I did not have a trace of Dharma, of peace and harmony. When I took the first step to experience the Dhamma, my entire outlook changed: I started feeling peace and harmony within and realised what a Dharmic person truly is.

Having experienced both situations, I am recommending that you spare ten days. You will not be wasting them; you will find that these were the best ten days of your life.

And once you find the path keep walking step by step, and reach the final goal of full liberation from the bondages of impurities and negativities, which make you miserable, so that you can enjoy real peace, real harmony, real happiness.

Dharma—
Its Definition and Universal Application

S. N. Tandon

In literary records the usage of the word *dharma* can be traced back to the Vedic times. The more prevalent form of the word, however, was *dharman*. Both these words are derived from a verbal root *dhṛ*,[1] which means to bear, support, sustain.

According to an old Indian tradition, the sages of the past witnessed Dharma, and then they transmitted it to those who had not witnessed it, through *mantras*[2]. This implies that the Dharma witnessed by the sages must have been something uncommon and exceptional, which had not fallen to the lot of the common man to witness.

A question would naturally arise as to what the sages witnessed that was so invaluable. From a careful reflection on the Vedic passages, it appears that they witnessed the nature or characteristic property of the various objects of the universe—whether animate or inanimate. This formed their realisation of Dharma, which they transmitted to later generations, through Vedic *mantras*.

The words *dharma* and *dharman* have had a chequered history as far as their usage in Indian literature is concerned. In the earlier period, these meant "support, law, truth, duty, manner, quality or characteristic". In the course of time, however, these came to have several other meanings, such as "religion, ethics, good works, the customary observances of a caste, sect, etc."

Examples of Usage of the Word "Dharma" in Literature

A study of Indian literature reveals that two main meanings of the word "dharma" have been preserved throughout the ages:

to sustain (its generic meaning, based on the word *dhṛ*), and

nature or characteristic (a specific meaning, based on realisation).

A few examples:-

* *Mitrā-varuṇā tvā paridhattāṃ dhruveṇa dharmaṇā.*[3]

May (the divine pair) *Mitra-Varuṇa* sustain thee with inviolable character.

* *Eṣa dharmo ya eṣa (sūryah) tapatyeṣa hīdaṃ sarvaṃ dhārayatyeteneva sarvaṃ dhṛtaṃ.*[4]

The blazing of the sun is its characteristic. This, verily, sustains all this. It is because of this that everything is sustained.

* *Dharmeṇa sarvamidaṃ parigṛhītam.*[5]

All this is sustained because of its nature.

* *Dhāraṇād dharmamityāhuh.*[6]

Dharma is called so because it sustains.

* *Dharmo vastusvabhāvah syāt.*[7]

Dharma means the nature of an object.

* *"Kusalā dhammā akusalā dhammā" ti ādisu sabhāvo attho.*[8]

In phrases such as "wholesome dharmas" and "unwholesome dharmas," the word "dharma" means nature.

* *Dhatte dharmah prajāh sarvāh.*[9]

Dharma sustains all beings.

* *Sahajo rūpatattvañca dharmah.*[10]

Dharma means natural quality of an object.

* *Dharmo' strī puṇya ācāre svabhāvopamayoh kratau.*[11]

Dharma, which is non-feminine, means merit, conduct, *nature*, comparison and sacrifice.

* *Dharmo' strī sukṛte sāmye svabhāve na tu somape.*[12]

Dharma, which is non-feminine, means good deeds, equanimity, *nature*, abstemiousness.

* *Dharmah svabhāvah ātmā syāt.*[13]

Dharma means *nature* as well as soul.

* *Dharmah vastuguṇarūpe svabhāve.*[14]

Dharma stands for the quality of a thing, its *nature*.

Thus, Dharma means the natural state or condition of beings and things, what sustains, the law of their being, what is right for them to be, the very stuff of their being.[15]

Limitations of the Vedas

There can hardly be any doubt that the Vedas are a repository of profound knowledge since they are based on the actual realisation of Dharma by the sages, but these do not serve the purpose of a common person for the following reasons:

archaic language;

no systematic exposition of Dharma which could appeal to the modern mind; and

absence of any living tradition which could lead its votaries to actual realisation of Dharma, like the primeval sages.

Dharma-Sūtra and Later Treatises

The oldest texts dealing directly with Dharma are known as the *Dharma-sūtras* (also called *Pūrva-mīmāṃsā*).[16] According to these, *dharma* means performance of duties in accordance with the Vedic injunctions. These devote themselves to the duties of castes and stages of life *(āśramas)*. Through these works one can clearly see an attempt on the part of the priestly class to transform the ancient laws for their own advantage, and to make their influence felt in all directions. Right from this stage, the universal character of Dharma, witnessed by the primeval sages, started losing its value because of its assuming a sectarian tinge.

The later treatises on Dharma, multifarious though they are,[17] are also not helpful in the proper understanding of Dharma for the following reasons:

their exposition of Dharma is not uniform;

they do not lay down clear, successive steps enabling a person to walk on the path of Dharma; and

there is no living tradition which could offset the above disadvantages.

All these treatises help in understanding Dharma only at the intellectual level, which does not meet the precise requirement of its actual realisation, as fulfilled by the primeval sages.

The *Bhagavadgītā*, popularly known as the "The Song Celestial", is reputed to contain the quintessence of the Upaniṣadic teaching. It is a marvellous composition widely acclaimed as a masterpiece for its lofty theme. It throws a flood of light on the various aspects of Dharma, including its practical aspects. However, this can also only be appreciated at the intellectual level, since there is no living tradition which could take it to the actual level where one can absorb the teaching.

It is only by the actual practice of Dharma that one can vanquish all sorts of mental impurities to become an enlightened person. When ignorance is dispelled from the mind, one realizes all sorts of dharmas and knows through insight the cause of each. Then all doubts are set at rest once and for all.[18] This happened in the case of Gotama the Buddha who, on reaching this stage, exclaimed with amazement, *Pubbe ananusuttesu dhammesu cakkhuṃ udapādi* [My eyes opened to dharmas that I had never heard before].[19]

A Living Tradition

The Tipiṭaka contains a detailed account of the various dharmas realised by the Buddha. If not for a living tradition which enables one to realize these dharmas at the actual (experiential) level, their mere presentation in the Tipiṭaka would have been as unproductive as their depiction in the Vedic *mantras.* Luckily such a living tradition is in existence, thanks to the chain of selfless, devoted teachers who preserved Dharma for posterity. All sorts of people, irrespective of their background, are taking advantage of it. A discussion on the dharmas spelt out by the Buddha would therefore be meaningful.

The Buddha's Exposition of Dharma

The Buddha's exposition of Dharma can be briefly stated as follows:

I. Dharma is infinite

Dharma means to bear, support, sustain.[20] It also means nature or characteristic.[21] Thus, Dharma is that which bears its own nature or characteristic.

There are two fields of existence: mundane and supra-mundane.

The entire mundane field from *Niraya-loka* to *Arūpa Brahma-loka* has the characteristic of impermanence. Also the fields of five aggregates (that is, all material and mental objects), six elements (earth, fire, water, air, ether and consciousness), and six bases (eye, ear, nose, tongue, skin and mind, and their own respective objects), all have this characteristic of impermanence.

Whatever is impermanent has the inherent characteristic of arising, passing away, decaying, dying. This leads to suffering.

The supra-mundane field lies outside the field of mind and matter. It is permanent in nature, and has the inherent characteristic of non-arising, non-decay, eternity, immortality. This leads to bliss.

Nothing lies beyond these two fields: mundane and supra-mundane. Each of them is governed by its own nature. In this sense, Dharma is all-pervasive. That is why it is said: *Appamāṇo dhammo* [Dharma is infinite].[22]

II. Dharma as a Mental Object

Whatever is borne by the mind at time constitutes its dharma during that period.

Just as the five senses—eye, ear, nose, tongue and skin—have for their objects vision, sound, smell, taste and touch respectively, so the mind as the sixth sense has dharmas for its object.[23]

The mental objects, called *cetasikas*, are of fifty-two types. These fall under two categories: *kusala* (wholesome) or *akusala* (unwholesome). A dharma qualifies to be called *kusala* if carrying it in the mind proves beneficial to its carrier, and it qualifies to be called *akusala* if carrying it in the mind proves otherwise (See Figure 1).

Likewise, some other words came into vogue, such as:

puñña dhamma (dharma by carrying which the mind becomes pure);

pāpa dhamma (dharma by carrying which the mind becomes impure);

sukka dhamma (dharma by carrying which the mind becomes bright);

kaṇha dhamma (dharma by carrying which the mind becomes dark);

ariya dhamma (dharma by carrying which the mind becomes noble);

anariya dhamma (dharma by carrying which the mind becomes ignoble); and so on.

III. Dharma as the Carrier of Wholesome Mental Factors

Prudence requires that one should carry in one's mind mental factors that are wholesome, beneficial and advantageous. This, for obvious reasons, is for one's own good. Hence, the word *dharma* came to be used in an exclusively good sense as well, the opposite being *adharma*.

IV. Dharma as Duty

Whatever proves fit to be carried in the mind should also prove fit to be carried out as one's duty. Conversely, whatever is not found fit to be carried in the mind cannot entail an obligation to carry it out as one's duty. Thus, one need not be expected to treat some nefarious design in the mind as one's duty. Hence Dharma came to be called duty, and *adharma,* non-duty.

The Buddha used to deliver sermons on both dharma and *adharma.*[24] He wanted people to understand what is wholesome or unwholesome, what is reproachable or irreproachable, what should be pursued or should not etc. He would exhort people to strive to abandon unwholesome dharmas and to acquire wholesome dharmas.[25]

V. Dharma as Universal Truth

Dharma means universal truth.[26] It refers to laws of nature or the nature of laws *(dhamma-niyāmatā).* In the Vedas this was called *ṛta.*[27] All laws of nature are of a permanent character.

Laws of Nature

Some of the laws enunciated by the Buddha are:

The Three Characteristics of Existence

"Whether enlightened persons appear in the world or not, it still remains a firm condition, an immutable fact and a fixed law that all formations are impermanent, all formations are subject to suffering and everything is without self."[28]

The Law of Cause and Effect

"If this is, that comes to be; from the arising of this, that arises; if this is not, that does not come to be; from the stopping of this, that is stopped."[29]

The Law of Causal Genesis

"With the base of ignorance, reaction arises; with the base of reaction, consciousness arises; with the base of consciousness, mind and body arise; with the base of mind and body, the six senses arise; with the base of the six senses, contact arises; with the base of contact, sensation arises; with the base of sensation, craving and aversion arise; with the base of craving and aversion, attachment arises; with the base of attachment, the process of becoming arises; with the base of the process of becoming, birth arises; with the base of birth, ageing and death arise, together with sorrow, lamentation, physical and mental suffering and tribulations. Thus arises the entire mass of suffering."[30]

This is the "forward order". The "reverse order" shows how this entire mass of suffering ceases to be.

No Solidity in the Material World

"The entire world is in flames,

the entire world is going up in smoke;

the entire world is burning,

the entire world is vibrating."[31]

Ancient laws are also recalled on certain occasions, e.g., "Hatred begets hatred, it can be vanquished only through love",[32] or "Truth, verily, is an immortal homily".[33] Such laws are called *sanātana* (i.e., of hereditary nature).[34]

Direct Realisation of Dharma by the Buddha

The various aspects of Dharma referred to above were not propounded by the Buddha on the basis of some speculation, hearsay or traditional belief. Each one of these was realized by him through a complete probe of the mind-matter phenomenon and by witnessing the truth that lay beyond. Thus, observing truth from the grossest to the subtlest, he spanned the entire mundane and supra-mundane fields, along with their characteristics, and *then* proclaimed that Dharma, comprising both these fields, is "infinite".

Similarly, he discovered that the mind always carries some object or the other, be it anger, hatred, illwill or loving-kindness, compassion, goodwill, and so on. He referred to these mental objects as dharma. Then he realized that mental objects such as anger, hatred and illwill have the characteristic of defiling the mind, making one miserable. He also realized that mental objects such as loving-kindness, compassion and goodwill have the characteristic of purifying the mind, making one cheerful. He called these mental objects *akusala* or *kusala,* as the case may be, on the basis of such realisations. It was not because of some blind belief or just to establish some sort of authority.

The Buddha never proclaimed anything unless he had actually realized it at the deepest level of his mind. In this respect he was like the primeval sages who had also witnessed Dharma directly and had then proclaimed it for posterity. The Buddha is also called a Great Sage *(mahesi).*[35]

The direct realisation of Dharma is no longer the monopoly of these sages. The technique of Vipassana meditation taught by the Buddha (stray references to which are traceable in the Vedas also)[36] is the main tool for truth realisation. This is now within reach of everybody because of the living tradition which has brought it to our doorsteps.

Definition Of Dharma

Keeping the foregoing discussion in mind, Dharma may be defined as the laws of nature or nature of laws which, when realised through insight, lead one gradually towards the goal of full liberation.

Three Essential Ingredients

This definition takes care of the following three essential ingredients of Dharma:

The focal point is laws of nature or nature of laws, cutting across all sectarianism.

These laws, or their nature, have to be realized through insight at the experiential level, thereby saving Dharma from being degraded into a mere intellectual game.

One should have the feeling of being led on to the final goal of full liberation, which will make one persevere on the path of Dharma.

Implications of this Definition

This definition will have the following implications:

On account of the practical nature of Dharma, one will be able to distinguish clearly between Dharma and religion, the latter being merely a profession of faith in some divinity or saintly person.[37]

On account of the element of self-introspection, one will not develop blind faith and one will always want to examine Dharma by the touchstone of one's own intuitive wisdom.[38]

One will come to realize the negligible value, or even utter futility, of rites and rituals.[39]

One will start realizing the fruits of Dharma here-and-now,[40] the most precious fruit being evenness of mind in all the vicissitudes of life.[41]

Reaping more and more rewards through applied Dharma, one will feel the urge to make Dharma one's refuge[42] in the real sense of the term.

One will no longer feel the necessity of remaining tied to a guru for all times to come.[43]

One will begin to appreciate the real intent of scriptural texts and age-old maxims and sayings.[44]

Distinctive Feature of Dharma

As already indicated, the distinctive feature of Dharma is that it should be capable of being realised at the experiential level through insight, and applied in daily life. Unless Dharma becomes applicable in daily life, it will be like a flower that is lovely and beautiful to look at, but does not emit any fragrance.[45]

With the proper application of Dharma in daily life, one is bound to get amazing results. When this starts happening, one begins to realise sooner rather than later that applied Dharma is nothing but an art of living, as it keeps one happy and contented in all situations.

Universal Application of Dharma

Although Dharma is universal and has nothing to do with sectarianism, the misconception that these are one and the same has prevailed in India for a long time. Even in the Buddha's time there were people who would use such terms as "my dharma" and "another's dharma":

> They call their own dharma perfect and the other's dharma imperfect. Thus contending, they quarrel with each other. They consider their own depositions to be true.[46]

To guard people against such statements, the Buddha gave a clear and succinct message to the Kālāmas, who also felt perturbed by similar talk on certain occasions:

> Now look, you Kālāmas. Be not misled by report or tradition or hearsay. Be not misled by proficiency in any scripture, or

by reasoning or logic or reflection on and approval of some theory, or because some view conforms with one's own inclinations, or out of respect for the prestige of a teacher. But when you *know for yourselves:* these things are unwholesome, these things are blameworthy, these things are censured by the wise; these things when practised and observed, conduce to loss and sorrow–then do ye reject them. But if at any time you *know for yourselves:* these things are wholesome, these things are praised by the intelligent; these things, when practised and observed, conduce to welfare and happiness, then Kālāmas, do ye, having practised them, abide.[47]

Thus, the accent in this message was on *realising for oneself* [48] for the sake of one's welfare. Such realisation comes through the practice of Vipassana, the technique of meditation taught by the Buddha. This technique is universal to the core, concerned solely with the practice of morality *(sīla),* mastery over the mind *(samādhi)* and insight *(paññā).*

Promotion of Dharma by Emperor Aśoka

Nearly two centuries after the passing away of the Buddha, the Emperor Aśoka tried this universal technique for the spiritual development of his people, with remarkable success. This earned him great fame in the annals of the world. H.G. Wells, the renowned historian of modern times, pays glowing tribute to him in the following words:

Amidst the tens of thousands of names of monarchs that crowd the columns of history, their majesties and graciousnesses and serenities and royal highnesses and the like, the name of Aśoka shines, and shines almost alone, a star.[49]

Emperor Aśoka explains in one of his edicts[50] how he could achieve amazing sucess while his predecessors could not. According to him, in olden times other rulers also wanted their subjects to progress by the adequate promotion of Dharma. He himself was filled with a similar desire, and to achieve this goal he undertook various measures. He provided several types of amenities to the public, as his predecessors had, but doing this proved of no avail. Then he exhorted people to follow certain dharma practices, so that they might develop compassion, charity, truthfulness, purity, gentleness and goodness. For this purpose he adopted two means: the issue of dharma proclamations and the practice of deep introspection *(nijhati).*

In fact, the exhortations to follow dharma practices proved of little avail; much more was accomplished through deep introspection. A forty-three-foot-high pillar, standing atop a three-storey citadel of Sultan Firioz Shah (1351–1388 A.D.) in Delhi, bears an inscription to this effect; this is eloquent testimony to the success of deep introspection in moulding the human character for the better (See Plates 1–3).

The Aśokan word *nijhati* corresponds to the Pāli word *nijjhatti,* occurring in the Tipiṭaka,[51] where it has been enumerated as a "strength". It means "deep introspection", or "insight", i.e, Vipassana. Thus Dharma, according to Aśoka, progressed in his time mainly because of Vipassana, taught by him to his people. For this purpose his approach was purely non-sectarian. The *Dharma-Mahāmātras,* the class of officers appointed by him for its propagation, approached *all* sections of society without any discrimination whatsoever. They occupied themselves with *all* sects of ascetics and householders.[52]

Proclamations versus Actual Practice

India today is trying to emulate the ideals of Aśoka: it has adopted the emblems that adorned his pillars everywhere, it is spreading messages of peace and goodwill to all other nations, it is resisting the temptation to engage in war even in the face of provocation, it is trying to use tolerance to deal with the spectre of fanaticism, its constitution provides for equality of all people before the law. But in spite of all this, the goal of peace and harmony is nowhere in sight.

The lacuna is obvious. Aśoka himself had realised the lacuna in his earlier attempts at ameliorating the lot of the people. He confessed that mere proclamations did not help. It was the actual practice of Dharma by the people that brought the desired results. Present-day India, or for that matter any country, can make its people happy and harmonious, with positive outlooks, by providing them with facilities for the actual practice of Dharma. Real happiness and harmony dawn only when people develop compassion, charity, truthfulness, purity, gentleness and goodness in themselves. Aśoka succeeded in inculcating these virtues amongst his people through the actual practice of Vipassana. The same results are bound to follow if this lacuna is removed in modern India.

History of the Vipassana Technique

Vipassana is one of India's most ancient meditation techniques. It contains the essence of what the Buddha practised and taught during his lifetime. In those days large numbers of people in northern India were freed from the bonds of suffering by practising Vipassana, and they attained high levels of achievement in all spheres of life. Over time, the technique spread to the neighbouring countries of Burma, Sri Lanka, Thailand and others, where it had the same ennobling effect.

Five centuries later, the noble heritage of Vipassana disappeared from India. The purity of the teaching was lost elsewhere as well. In Burma, however, it was preserved by a chain of devoted teachers. From generation to generation, for over two thousand years, this dedicated lineage has transmitted the technique in its pristine purity.

In our time, Vipassana has been reintroduced to India, as well as to citizens of more than eighty other countries, by Shri S.N. Goenka, who was authorised to teach Vipassana by the renowned Burmese Vipassana teacher Sayagyi U Ba Khin. In India ten-day Vipassana courses have been held since 1969, and in other countries since 1979. During this short span of time nearly thirty centres have been established worldwide, to enable people to practise Vipassana exclusively. Thus ever-increasing numbers of people are getting the opportunity to learn this art of living, which brings lasting peace and happiness to people from all walks of life.

A Non-Sectarian Technique

Although Vipassana was rediscovered and taught by the Buddha, it cannot be termed "Buddhist". The Buddha never called his followers Buddhists, he called them *dhammaṭṭha*[53] (dharma wayfarers). The technique contains nothing of a sectarian nature, and it can be accepted and applied by people of any background. The basis of the technique is the recognition that all human beings share the same problems, and that a pragmatic method which can eradicate these problems can be universally practised.

Vipassana courses are open to anyone sincerely wishing to learn the technique irrespective of race, caste, faith or nationality. Hindus, Muslims, Sikhs, Jains, Buddhists, Christians, Jews, as well as members of other religions, have all successfully completed Vipassana courses. Besides permanent centres, courses are also held in schools, colleges, universities, hostels, libraries, *panchayatwadis*, *dharmaśālās*, temples, mosques, churches, nunneries, *vihāras*, *upāśrayas*, *aśramas*, hotels, jails, etc.[54] People from all backgrounds who practise Vipassana find that they become better human beings.

Impressed by these results, the Government of India has lately decided to introduce Vipassana in prisons. In 1994, the largest Vipassana course to date, for over one thousand prison inmates, was held in Tihar Jail, Delhi, which happens to be the biggest prison in Asia in terms of its population. The course proved to be remarkable in many ways. The prison inmates confessed openly that it was a unique experience for them and that they felt a distinct change for the better in their behaviour patterns. Similar courses are now being held in other prisons as well, and the demand for such courses is constantly on the increase.

Now Vipassana has come to be recognised as an unfailing instrument for dealing with all sorts of ills of present-day society. It is looked upon as a means for human uplift. Dharma, too, has all through the ages been looked upon as an unfailing instrument for human uplift. In this respect, Vipassana and Dharma should appear to be one and the same. But the difference lies in the fact that while one gets all the good results from Vipassana, one does not get these from Dharma. This is because Dharma has lost its universal character and become sectarian. Once its universal character is restored, it will also start giving all the benefits expected from it.

The Universal Character of Vipassana or Dharma

The universal character of Vipassana or Dharma lies in "self-introspection", for which the Enlightened One proclaimed:

> All those who, in the past, purified their deeds of body, speech and mind did so only through self-introspection *(paccavekkhaṇa);*
>
> all those who, in the future, will purify their deeds of body, speech and mind, will do so only through self-introspection; and
>
> all those who, in the present, are purifying their deeds of body, speech and mind are doing so only through self-introspection.[55]

BHAVATU SABBA MAṄGALAṂ

References

1. Dharma (masc. & neut.) - from dhṛ + man (suffix) [*dharati lokān, dhriyate puṇyātmabhiriti vā*] (Halāyudha-kośa, ed. Jayaśaṅkara Jośī) Also, "*dhāraṇāt dharma*" (Sāyaṇa on Ṛgveda, 3.17.1)
2. "*sākṣātkṛtadharmāṇa ṛṣayo babhūvuste 'varebhyo' sākṣātkṛtadharmabhya upadeśena mantrān saṃprāduh*" (Nirukta by Yāska)
3. Maitrāyaṇī saṃhitā (4.9.1)
4. Śatapatha-brāhmaṇa (Mādhyandinīya) (14.2.2.29)
5. Taittirīya- āraṇyaka (10.62.1)

6. Mahābhārata (Śāntiparva, 108/11)
7. Jain Lakṣaṇāvalī
8. Itivuttaka-aṭṭhakathā, ed. Dr Nathamal Tatia (p. 47)
9. Brahmāṇḍa-mahāpurāṇa, ed. Dr K.B. Sharma (p. 19)
10. Abhidhāna-cintāmaṇi, ed. Pt. Hargovind Śāstrī
11. Medinī-kośa, ed. Pt. Jagannātha Śāstrī
12. Vaijayantī-kośa, ed. Pt. Hargovind Śāstrī
13. Halāyudha-kośa, ed. Jayaśaṅkara Jośī (782)
14. Śabdastoma-mahānidhi
15. Majjhima-nikāya, Vol. I (PTS edn.) (p. xix)
16. The difficult nature of these texts can be visualized from the Preface appearing in the English translation of the Sūtras: "The translator knows how difficult it was to understand the Mīmāṃsā in interpreting the Vedic rituals of the ancient Aryans and is still not sure whether he has correctly explained them." (Mīmāṃsā Sūtras of Jaimini; pub. Motilal Banasidas.)
Obviously Dharma expounded in texts, which are not even intelligible to scholars, can be of little use to ordinary people.
17. For example, those of Manu, Yājñavalkya, Kāśyapa, Baudhāyana, Nārada, Hārīta, Uśanas, Aṅgīras, Yama, Atri, Saṃvarta, Dakṣa, Śātātapa, Śaṅkha, Kātyāyana, Gautama, Bṛhaspati and so on.
18. "*Yadā have pātubhavanti dhammā, ātāpino jhāyato brāhmaṇassa; athassa kaṅkhā vapayanti sabbā yato pajānāti sahetu-dhammaṃ*" (Udāna-pāli, 1.1.2)
19. Saṃyutta-nikāya, 12.4.5
20. "*dhāretīti dhammo*"
21. "*dhamma-saddo pakati-pariyāyo.*" (Mahāvagga-ṭīkā on Dīgha-nikāya 1.17.17)
22. Aṅguttara-nikāya, 4.7.7
23. "*manañca paṭicca dhamme uppajjati viññāṇaṃ, manoviññāṇaṃ tveva saṅkhaṃ gacchati.*" (Majjhima-nikāya, I.38.2.5)
24. "*dhammaṃ ca vo, bhikkave, desessāmi, adhammaṃ ca.*" (Aṅguttara-nikāya, 10.14.5)
25. "*āraddhaviriyo viharati akusalānaṃ dhammānaṃ pahānāya, kusalānaṃ dhammānaṃ uppādāya.*" (Majjhima-nikāya, II.35.5.25)
26. "*saccapariyāyo hi ... dhamma-saddo.*" (Pāthikavagga-ṭīkā on Dīgha-nikāya, 10.331)
27. "*ṛtasya dhītirvṛjināni hanti*" (Thought of Eternal Law removes transgressions.) (Ṛgveda, 4.23.8)
28. "*uppādā vā tathāgatānaṃ anuppādā vā tathāgatānaṃ ṭhitā va sā dhātu dhammaṭṭhitatā dhammaniyāmatā idappaccayatā... 'sabbe saṅkhārā aniccā' ti; 'sabbe saṅkhārā dukkhā' ti; 'sabbe dhammā anattā' ti.*" (Aṅguttara-nikāya, 3.14.4)
29. "*iti imasmiṃ sati idaṃ hoti, imassuppādā idaṃ uppajjati; imasmiṃ asati idaṃ na hoti, imassa nirodhā idaṃ nirujjhati.*" (Saṃyutta-nikāya, 12.21.22)
30. "*avijjā-paccayā saṅkhārā; saṅkhāra-paccayā viññāṇaṃ; viññāṇa-paccayā nāmarūpaṃ; nāmarūpa-paccayā saḷāyatanaṃ; saḷāyatana-paccayā*

phasso; phassa-paccayā vedanā; vedanā-paccayā taṇhā; taṇhā-paccayā upādānaṃ; upādāna-paccayā bhavo; bhava-paccayā jāti; jāti-paccayā jarā-maraṇaṃ-soka-parideva-dukkha-domanassupāyāsā sambhavanti. Evametassa kevalassa dukkhakhandhassa samudayo hoti." (Majjhima-nikāya, I.38.3.9)

31. "*sabbo ādīpito loko... sabbo loko pakampito.*" (Saṃyutta-nikāya, 5.7.7)

32. "*na hi verena verāni, sammantīdha kudācanaṃ; averena hi sammanti, esa dhammo sanantano.*" (Dhammapada, 1.1.5)

33. "*saccaṃ va amatā vācā, esa dhammo sanantano.*" (Sutta-nipāta, 3.3.49)

34. "*dhammoti sanantano paveṇīdhammo.*" (Sīlakkhandhavagga-abhinavaṭīkā 2.2.162)

35. Abhidhānappadīpikā, ed. Waskaḍuwé Subhūti, Colombo (2.1033)

36. for example, "*yo viśvābhi vipaśyati bhuvanā saṃ ca paśyati, sa nah parṣadati dviṣah.*" (Atharva-veda, 6.34.4)

37. Oxford Advanced Learner's Dictionary, Oxford University:
"Religion: 1. Belief in the existence of God or gods, who has/have created the universe and given man a spiritual nature which continues to exist after the death of the body. 2. Particular system of faith and worship based on such a belief, the Christian, Buddhist and Hindu religions."

38. "*dhammoti paññā*" (Sumaṅgala-vilāsinī, III.5.150)

39. Refer to Aśoka's Rock Edict IX.

40. "*sandiṭṭhiko-akāliko*' (Dīgha-nikāya, 2.3.159)

41. "*phuṭṭhassa lokadhammehi, cittaṃ yassa na kampati*" (Khuddaka-pāṭho, 5.11)

42. "*dhamma-saraṇo*" (Dīgha-nikāya, 2.3.165)

43. "*atta-saraṇo*" (Dīgha-nikāya, 2.3.165)

44. for example, "*ārogya-paramā lābhā, nibbānaṃ paramaṃ sukhaṃ*" (Health is the highest gain, Nirvāṇa is the highest bliss.) (Majjhima-nikāya, II.25.2.10-14)

45. "*yathā pi ruciraṃ pupphaṃ, vaṇṇavantaṃ agandhakaṃ; evaṃ subhāsitā vācā, aphalā hoti akubbato.*" (Dhammapada, 4.51)

46. "*sakaṃ hi dhammaṃ paripuṇṇamāhu,
aññassa dhammaṃ pana hīnamāhu;
evaṃ pi viggahya vivādayanti,
sakaṃ sakaṃ sammutimāhu saccaṃ.*"
(Mahāniddesa-pāḷi, 1.13.139)

47. "*Etha tumhe, kālāmā, mā anussavena, mā paramparāya, mā itikirāya, mā piṭakasampadānena, mā takkahetu, mā nayahetu, mā ākāra-parivitakkena, mā diṭṭinijjhānakkhantiyā, mā bhabbarūpatāya, mā samaṇo no garū ti. Yadā tumhe, kālāmā, attanā va jāneyyātha—ime dhammā akusalā, ime dhammā sāvajjā, ime dhammā viññu-garahitā, ime dhammā samattā samādinnā ahitāya dukkhāya saṃvattantī'ti, atha tumhe, kālāma, pajaheyyātha......yadā tumhe, kālāmā, attanā va jāneyyātha—'ime dhammā kusalā, ime dhammā anavajjā, ime dhammā viññuppasatthā, ime dhammā samattā samādinnā hitāya sukhāya saṃvattantī' ti, atha tumhe, kālāmā, upasampajja vihareyyātha.*" (Aṅguttara-nikāya, 3.7.5)

48. "*paccattaṃ veditabbo hi dhammo.*" (Dīgha-nikāya, 2.8.354)

49. The Outline History of the World, by H.G. Wells
50. Delhi-Topra Pillar Edict VII
51. Paṭisambhidāmagga, 2.9.1.2; 2.9.2.16
52. Delhi-Topra Pillar Edict VII
53. "*dhammassa gutto medhāvī, dhammaṭṭho ti pavuccati.*" (The intelligent one protected by Dharma is called "*dhammaṭṭho*".) (Dhammapada, 19.257)
54. Sayagyi U Ba Khin Journal, V.R.I. (p. 295–303)
55. Majjhima-nikāya, II.11.2.6

Discussion Extracts

After the learned discourse by Goenkaji and then further elucidation by Tandonji, I find myself in a great dilemma to say something on Dharma. But I will ask just this: When does this question arise? When do you ask the question: "What is Dharma?" That itself is a big question, because unless you ask this question, you can never know about Dharma.

The question comes after the needs of survival and procreation have been met. It comes when you have achieved a certain level of success or you have failed; then you ask "What is it? Why am I ... What is this existence?" and so on. When these questions arise then you try to find the answer.

But every time you try to find out you go for a shortcut. That shortcut is to believe in what others say. You ask your parents, or the gurus of your family, birth or sect—the easiest way—and you believe that you are Dharmic as Goenkaji said.

Just as there is a large number of people who believe they are Dharmic, there is also a large number of people known as non-Dharmic or adharmic.

Now, in the so called Dharmic category, those who say "We believe in this and this gospel or scripture" are again of two types. One type will say that they know it after reading or understanding, and there are others who believe it because it has been said by the guru or the head of a sect.

But of the so-called non-Dharmic people, there are three types. The first says, "I do not believe in anything like rebirth or god or whatever the scriptures say"; the second says, "I do not know"; and the third says, "I do not want to know." Now, those who do not want to know, you can't help them; but those who do not know, at least they can try to know. But one who says "I do not believe" is free to learn or start thinking.

The trouble is with those who say "We know, and we believe." They have a lot to unlearn, and that causes a big problem.

Now, when you start asking the question "Why am I here? What is my object in life?" and so on, this itself is the fundamental question of life, which leads to inquiry into Dharma.

Those who fall into the trap of believing or following a certain sect or religion cannot rise in their level of consciousness. We all do many things unawares, many things by instinct, many things as animals would do, but once you are aware of your actions and feelings, only then can you know what is said.

Now this is the reason why Vipassana or meditation becomes important: you become conscious of yourself, you don't have to believe what others say, but you have to know what is your feeling, what it is that you want, what it is that you have to achieve. If you know this, then the principles of life and rules of good conduct come to you automatically. You don't have to be taught and no enforcement machinery is necessary.

As Tandonji mentioned, Aśoka found it necessary to make people realise these things in order to enforce the law, rather than impose it by punishment. Unfortunately in our educational system people are not trained to raise questions. When they are trained, they are given information, they are asked to remember and reproduce it. There is no time to think, there is no time to reflect. That is why we have people who know, but people who do not realise, people who are not aware.

Mr R.S. Kumat, I.A.S.
Chairman of the Board of Revenue
Rajasthan

The speakers so far have been talking about what is truth, what is Vipassana, what is Dharma, and how to live a life of Dharma. These issues are not being discussed for the first time on the Indian subcontinent. Everybody has different views because of the variety in our tastes, our likings, but all of us have to reach the same destination, like rivers meeting the ocean. This is our ancient heritage and this heritage has given a great quality of tolerance to the subcontinent. It is extremely unfortunate that today we see a decay in this value. Hence this seminar is very important.

As long as one does not make an effort to know oneself, one cannot progress or become liberated from the lower realms of life. I am very happy that we have gathered here to learn about Vipassana.

Mr Madan Mani Dixit
Vice Chancellor
Royal Nepal Academy

I have had the impression, and maybe it's a mistaken impression, that in some of the talks there was a kind of dismissal of religion as being sectarian. Maybe I am mistaken in having this impression, but I would like to take this occasion firstly to say a word for these religions, and secondly to make an appeal for the right kind of religion we need today.

Religions have been said—whether here or in other places—to be sectarian. I think we have to admit that there is a multiplicity of religions, and that there are real differences between religions. But I think that is different from saying that religions are sectarian. Sectarian means that we see our religion as the sole repository of truth, that we exclude other religions, and we are not open to them.

I want to make an appeal for this openness. Religions are different, and multifarious. I would admit that they are, in practice, to some extent sectarian. All the main religions mention the family of humankind and that God wanted all men to be one family. So they don't want their message to go only to one particular group of people. Religions need not be sectarian, although they may hold that they are the path which they think is the right path for all.

I think it is dangerous to stress this sectarianism of religion because it could lead to indifference to religions. In my opinion we cannot be indifferent to religions, we have to be committed to them.

This is the UN Year of Tolerance, and therefore I think it is the year when we could renew our attitude to the other religions. For some time now I have been taking part in meetings between members of different faiths, trying to encourage an inter-religious dialogue. In 1994 I was pleased to attend a UNESCO conference in Barcelona, also attended by the Dalai Lama, on this very theme. The representatives of all religions sat together to discuss what we felt to be a common challenge: to go back to our sources and promote peace worldwide rather than war. It was agreed that between us we could mobilise considerable material and spiritual resources for the good of humanity. This declaration should be widely publicised and supported so that it can be submitted to the UN. We should accept that there is a lot of truth in the other religions, and that we have a lot to receive from them also. I think, and this is my message, that to be religious in today's world, to be religious in a country as rich as India is in religious legacies, is to be inter-religious. To be closed is not really to be truly religious.

Father Aelred Pereira
Mumbai

The real Dhamma teaches us unity in diversity. To adopt the way of inner understanding, the training and taming of mind is essential. For that Vipassana can help us.

Mr Vidyaadhar Gokhale
Journalist, Mumbai

I have been listening to people talking about their experiences of Vipassana. Whatever I have heard about Vipassana has been inspiring for me.

Corruption and organised gangs are common today. For our society to become a better society, every person has to look at himself and improve himself. Dharma teaches us to become good citizens ourselves.

Another thing I would like to mention is the great job done by women in our society. They have been at the forefront of the moral upliftment and now if they are involved more and more in Vipassana, the future of our country will become bright.

Mr. G. R. Khairnar
Mumbai

Clarifications have been requested from two quarters, and I will attempt to answer them.

Mr H.E. Dhagat has written, "Have I heard you correctly, that Gotama said that there is nothing beyond the sensory field for understanding Dharma? Is it not true that human life on a higher plane is always an effort to reach beyond the sensory field? If so, please reconcile the apparent contradiction in what Gotama seems to have said. Perhaps I may have heard wrongly, in which case, please elucidate the statement."

A very short time was allotted, so I will now explain in slightly greater detail. The Buddha said that Dharma is infinite. It is unfathomable. I mentioned that there are two fields of existence: mundane and supramundane. The entire mundane field has the characteristic of impermanence, as do the fields of five aggregates—that is, all material and mental objects. So do the six elements (earth, fire, water, air, ether, and consciousness) and the six bases (eye, ear, nose, tongue, skin, and mind, and their respective sense objects). All have the characteristics of impermanence. This is the mundane field. And whatever is impermanent has the inherent characteristic of arising, passing away, decaying, dying, and this leads to suffering.

Now, when we come to the supramundane field, it lies outside the field of mind and matter. It is permanent in nature and it has the inherent characteristic of non-arising, non-decay, eternity, immortality. This leads to bliss. The Buddha had spanned both fields: he had experienced both the mundane field from niraya loka to arūpa-brahma loka and the supramundane field. He felt that nothing lies beyond these two fields, that is, mundane and supramundane. Keeping this in view he mentioned that each one of these is governed by its own nature, whether of permanence or impermanence. So in this sense Dharma is all-pervasive. That is why he said appamāno dhammo, that is, Dharma is infinite. So this is regarding the query raised by Mr Dhagat.

Also, Professor Tiwary has raised certain points about the definition of the word dharma. We find that in the aṭṭhakathās—that is the commentaries on the Tipiṭaka—it is written many times: *Dhāreti ti dhammo* [that which is sustained is dharma.]

Going to the Indo-European period, this word dharma in Sanskrit is firm in Latin. "Firm" in English comes from firmamen in Latin. So dharma and "firm" both have the same characteristic: they are stable, permanent, not changing.

Another point was regarding the meaning "law of nature" ascribed to the word dharma. I feel that labels are not important, it is the contents that are important. The various laws that have been enunciated by Buddha, for example: whatever arises also has the nature of passing away; everything is impermanent. Many similar laws were enunciated by him. And he himself says: "I am dhammakāyo. These are all the Dhammas, I am an aggregate of all these. Once you see all these things in me, you are seeing Dhamma." What he is propounding is only these universal laws. And he wants us to see him in this light only.

On the basis of our own realisation of Dharma, on the basis of Vipassana, we find the laws of nature enunciated by the Buddha to be true. We can only call them "dharma" in the widest sense of the term, that this supports us. It is on the basis of these dharmas that we can lead a happy and contented life.

Mr S.N. Tandon
Delhi

I thought I could mention two or three interesting points. The first point is whether there is a conflict between religion and Dharma. By stressing Dharma are we saying that religions become unimportant? I won't belabour that point, but I was reminded of a Sufi saint who lived in the earlier part of this century. He was speaking about spiritualism in general and saying that truth is universal. Somebody asked him "Why is it that you belong to the Islamic religion?" He said: "We need a vehicle for achieving the truth. Religion is the vehicle for achieving the truth, and it makes little difference whether you are taking the vehicle of Islam, or the vehicle of Christianity, or the vehicle of Hinduism. Ultimately the vehicle will lead you to the same path, namely, the Truth." I think that is a very perceptive observation which makes me believe that one need not be irreligious to follow the Dharma; I don't think that there is a basic conflict.

The second point is about the question of religious tolerance, which was mentioned. There was a great leader who lived in the later part of the last century, Swami Vivekananda. When somebody asked him about religious tolerance, he said he didn't believe in religious tolerance at all. He said that the word is a misnomer and that we should not encourage this concept of religious tolerance, because tolerance means that you are superior and you are tolerating some other religion. I think I will substitute the phrase "religious acceptance", in the sense that only the finder of the truth will realise that all religions are the same. In the sense that all the rivers lead to the ocean, I think that a degree of acceptance on the part of an individual is required that the religions are the same.

The third point that I want to stress is that we should not give too much importance to words and meanings. Ultimately, all the words have the meaning which we ascribe to them. Once you know the substance, words become irrelevant because they have no meaning in the dimension in which we are operating.

The final question I will ask is: To what extent will the following of Dharma be in conflict with whatever we do in society, and can Dharma and society be integrated? But that will be the subject of the next session. In fact Goenkaji started by saying that pure Dharma is not of relevance unless it is applicable in modern life.

Mr N. Vaghul, Chairman
Industrial Credit and Investment Corp.
Mumbai

Dharma—Its Role in Current Social Problems

Sally McDonald

Introduction

There have always been social problems, ranging from simple family or village disputes to tribal conflicts, and then later to state rivalries and international wars. There have always been individuals who suffer from unhealthy surroundings, or from discrimination, seemingly unfair burdens of misery and oppression, and who react with fear and mistrust. There have always been individuals and groups who try to change or repair the wrongs of society, and at times despair that anything can be done.

All of these problems start with the same cause: the forces of hatred, greed and ignorance that exist in all of our individual minds. It is therefore at the individual level that the solution lies.

We can define Dharma as a scientific path of self-introspection and wisdom, of not reacting with negativity and of cultivating positive mental qualities instead. To succeed, it involves diligent practice, not just theorising and discussion.

The role of Dharma in current social problems therefore appears to be threefold:

1. to eliminate the mental defilements that cause us to do wrong, so that we do not add to the problems and suffering in our society;
2. to help us bear the stress of competitiveness, crowded or polluted environments, and (for those who are less fortunate) the seeming injustices of life; and
3. to give us strength to serve and improve our society.

When the individuals in society do not follow the path of Dharma, the path of wisdom, then ignorance prevails and all the social ills are bound to come into play.

What Is New?

Today the world is a very different place from the world of even one hundred years ago. The problems we face are aggravated by the following:

* The sheer size of the world's population, especially in developing countries such as India, China and the African nations.
* The increasingly global nature of economics and politics, so that problems in one country have repercussions in the countries where they trade or wield power.
* The complexity of modern technology, especially that of modern warfare. This means that those individuals who understand and control this technology have unprecedented power.
* Huge changes in how we communicate: faster and easier local, national and international telephone, fax and computer links, plus mass-media news and entertainment.

* The rapid rate of change in how we work. This has led to increased competitiveness and stress in the workplace, and greater pressure on students in universities and schools. Physical and mental health suffer as a result.
* An increase in the number of social outcasts, who populate the world's slums, jails and psychiatric institutions.

All of these mean that there is an even greater need for solutions, solutions which involve flexible, intelligent, clear, and compassionate thinking. We need solutions which require not only knowledge and resources but, more important, wisdom.

Let us look at some of our current responses to these problems and how they can be improved by applying the principles of Dharma.

Improving on Current Responses

Existing Social Structures which Provide Moral Support

The traditional social institutions of family, schools and religious groups have always had a role in providing moral support and guidance. Their diminishing influence is often blamed on the lack of respect in today's youth, and the youth in turn blame the older generation for its inflexibility and clinging to old-fashioned ways.

The faults on both sides are outcomes of the same mental defilement: craving, along with its offspring attachment. If the youth of today can be educated in the science of pure Dharma instead of narrow, sectarian beliefs, they will naturally cultivate respect for those who teach them. They can also realise for themselves the danger in the endless pursuit of new experiences, and learn contentment. Likewise, the older generation can learn from pure Dharma the futility of clinging to rites and rituals.

We should use such education to strengthen our existing social support structures, rather than try to replace them with remedial institutions.

A German meditator who is a school-teacher has taught his class of fifteen-year-olds the technique of Anapana meditation, which is mindfulness of respiration. He said that instead of taking ten minutes for the class to stop laughing, shouting, banging desks, and finally settle down to listen to him, they now do five minutes of meditation, then quietly take out their books and immediately start the day's lesson.

Social Welfare and Remedial Institutions.

Although it is preferable to foster a society in which the individuals are responsible for their own well-being, we also need safetynets to help those who have fallen by the wayside, and those who have been discriminated against. There are many reactions to the pressures of modern life. Some seek escape in the madness of material desire, and fall into debt and despair. Others seek the mental void of alcohol and drugs. Others react with violence, vandalism and crime.

As mentioned above, the role of Dharma in solving such problems is threefold. First: it helps to remove the underlying defilements that create such reactions. Second: It helps the less fortunate to bear their suffering. Third: it strengthens those involved in helping such people, the social workers, doctors and so on.

One example is in the area of prison reform. The historic courses in Tihar Jail have already been mentioned. Discipline has improved and there is greater harmony between the inmates and staff, as representatives of both have learned the technique of self-introspection. A psychological study by the Department of Psychiatry of the All India Institute of Medical Sciences is in progress. Early results show that meditation reduces hostility and helplessness and leads to enhanced well-being and hope.[1] The Inspector General of Tihar has encouraged the prisoners not only to improve themselves, but to become useful members of society when they are released.

Other examples can be found in the area of drug rehabilitation. Proven results in treating drug addicts in Australia have been reported at a previous seminar.[2] A very successful program called "Start Again" is now under way in Switzerland, managed by several meditators. Because of its achievements in the past three years, funding has been increased and the program has been expanded considerably.

Legislation, Law and Order

There are so many laws now which attempt to restrict anti-social human activities. As well as the old codes which outlaw murder, rape, stealing and cheating, there are increasing complex laws about the use and distribution of drugs, about business ethics, patents and copyrights, and so on. In many countries, there are detailed laws trying to stop racial discrimination or casteism, and to promote equal opportunities for women. There are so many examples where these laws fail, even when they are diligently enforced. "All the upbeat formulations in the world cannot disguise the distortions and inefficiences that affirmative action programmes have failed to address and, in some cases, have helped to create."[3]

Naturally, it helps to have some guidelines, but we cannot force anyone to be inherently moral or compassionate towards others by making laws. Again, the answer lies at the individual level. There has to be a way that people learn to follow the spirit rather than just the letter of the law. The foundation of Dharma is morality, but it is only by developing mental clarity that we can fully comprehend its importance.

A young American woman did a ten-day course here in India recently, during this hot season. She had been sitting still and meditating for about half an hour, and felt a lot of heat and pain in her body. Then a mosquito came buzzing around her head. A thought came about killing the mosquito. She noticed that now the heat was almost unbearable, and that the pain had intensified, and realised that this was the result of her anger. She had understood for herself how we increase our own misery when we think of harming other beings.

Such insights naturally help individuals to stop causing harm, and also to develop compassion towards other suffering beings. This is the only way that society can become more law-abiding and more tolerant, not by making more laws about how to behave.

Science and Technology

There have been great strides in medical research to alleviate human suffering due to disease and old age. There have been improvements in agricultural methods and in communications. In many countries, people live longer, lead more comfortable lives and also have more leisure time. However, the benefits of science are matched by the disadvantages: by the stresses of modern life we have already mentioned, and by environmental degradation and pollution.

Mass-media news reporting has led to greater awareness of the world's problems, but mass-media "entertainment" has often degenerated into senseless promotion of violence and sexual fantasy, that is, to mental pollution. Multi-national corporations have seized this tool of communication to promote consumerism and to enhance their wealth and power.

What is needed is pure volition and wisdom in applying this new knowledge. Scientists and the users of their machines and techniques need to also study Dharma, to study their own mental and material phenomena, their own motives and actions, as well as studying the material world.

Powerful World Organisations

The horrifying problems of racial tension and terrorism, the recent nightmares we are hearing about in Africa, the ongoing poverty in so many parts of the world, are not going to be overcome easily. Powerful organisations with multi-million-dollar resources such as the United Nations and the World Bank have been unable to solve most of these problems. The USA, the remaining superpower, is at present evaluating its relationship with the rest of the post–Cold War world.[4] There is a growing reluctance in many of its citizens to get involved in foreign problems it has been unable to solve by military or economic means.

There is limited benefit in trying to change "the system" using political or welfare measures, when the underlying human defilements such as anger, craving and fear continue to exist. In any organisation, large or small, humanitarian aims will not be properly served if the people in it, especially the leaders, are working with narrow-minded, selfish interests and prejudices. Changes therefore must start in small ways, first in individuals, and then in groups of people who try to co-operate and incorporate the principles of Dharma in their lives and work. Later on, as the teaching of pure Dharma spreads, we can expect to see larger organisations applying the wisdom of Dharma in improving the world.

Breaking Down the Barriers

The practice of Vipassana meditation is now spreading throughout the world, and there is a great deal of international co-operation involved. At all of the Vipassana centres, people come from different states and different countries to give service for the benefit of others. Goenkaji and assistant teachers from India have conducted Vipassana courses in the West, and now you will find assistant teachers from Western countries conducting courses in Indonesia or Israel. The meditators from Western Europe have organised courses in former socialist countries, and have started a fund for courses in Africa. Other funds have been set up in the West to help the struggling nations in Southeast Asia, where the demand for courses is enormous, and in South America.

About 25,000 people attend courses in India each year, and about 8,000 in the rest of the world. They come from all walks of life. There are business and community leaders who try to incorporate the principles of Dharma in their organisations.[5] Eleven thousand schoolchildren attended courses last year.[6] You will also see uneducated village women and the poorer classes starting to come to Dhamma Giri. They often cannot give much for a donation; it is a struggle for them to pay their train fare to Igatpuri, yet somehow all the centres keep growing. The growth rate is about 20 to 25 per cent each year.

If this growth continues, there is a tremendous potential to break down many long-standing historical barriers, racial, social and economic. However, it must be said again, change must come at the individual level; all must take responsibility. Sometimes there are even more problems when our aim is for the good of society. Even when our volition is good, we have to face our own weaknesses whilst fighting against prejudice, greed and resistance to change in society. For this, great strength is needed.

By incorporating pure Dharma in our lives, we develop in confidence, in determination in our efforts, in awareness, in concentration, and in wisdom and equanimity. If we use these strengths in helping pure Dharma to spread, others will also find out how to break down the barriers of their mental impurities. In this way, all the barriers of intolerance and distrust in society can be broken, to establish greater peace and harmony in the world.

References

1. K Chandirimani, S.K. Verma, P.L. Dhar & N. Aggarwal, "Psychological Effects of Vipassana on Tihar Jail Inmates: A Preliminary Report", Vipassana—Its Relevance to the Modern World, an International Seminar, April 1994. Vipassana Research Institute, Igatpuri.
2. Hammersley, R & Cregan, J, "Drug Addiction and Vipassana Meditation", Seminar on Vipassana Meditation, May 1987, Vipassana Research Institute, Igatpuri.
3. "Affirmative Action—But some are more equal than others", The Economist, April 15th 1995, London.
4. Ogden, C., "Uncle Sam Hunkers Down", International Time Magazine, April 17th, 1995. New York.
5. Shah, J., "Vipassana and Business Management" Vipassana—Its Relevance to the Modern World, an International Seminar, April 1994. Vipassana Research Institute, Igatpuri.
6. Vipassana Annual Conference Report, January 1995. Vipassana Research Institute, Igatpuri.

Discussion Extracts

We are working in Rajasthan in a programme which is called 'Lok Jumbish', where we are trying to undertake the reconstruction of primary education, the education of children from Class One to Class Eight. We have found, as everybody here knows, that the most important factor is the teachers. Although Vipassana is very popular in Rajasthan, we in Lok Jumbish and in the organised educational system, have not been able to do much so far. However we have now decided that we will take up a community development block which has about 450 teachers. Those of us who have not yet experienced Vipassana will undergo a course and then talk to all the teachers of this block and persuade them to come to a Vipassana course. This should bring about a change in their own lifestyle, in the manner in which they deal with children, with parents; the aim is to create an environment in which we can nurture a new generation of children who are full of good qualities and self-confidence.

Mr Anil Bordia, I.A.S. (Ret'd)
Former Secretary of Education
Government of India

❦❦❦

As Goenkaji said in the morning, most of us sitting here are from the kindergarten. I would like to think myself a mere toddler as far as this technique of meditation is concerned.

So far as I can recollect, ever since I discovered myself, I have never done anything except playing cricket and even today my life revolves around cricket, and that in very simple words is Dharma for me.

Cricket is a way of life and I see so much similarity with Vipassana. Both involve applying a fairly consistent amount of concentration and effort over a period of time. When we say that someone is not playing cricket, it means that he is not being fair in life, he is not upright, he is not honest.

If I may cite an example, it is a quote from the late Prime Minister of Australia, Sir Robert Menzies, who once said: "If only America and Russia played cricket, this world would be a much happier place to live in."

I was talking to Mr Tandon, who first introduced me to this technique, and I said, whatever you are trying to teach us here—well I have already done a three-day course and I am going for a ten-day course in July—I call this a "psyching process", to peak up yourself at the right moment. I had many limitations with my own cricketing ability and I can tell you—people like Sunil Gavaskar and Kapil Dev—how they psyched themselves up for their performance, and then had pride in their personal achievements. When I say "pride", that should not be taken in a sense of conceit or arrogance. This "pride" means satisfaction at your personal performance. If you are not proud of yourself, I am afraid, nobody else is going to be proud of you. And this personal pride should be followed by something called national pride.

Personally I have learnt life is a never-ending process of learning, and I have learnt from Vipassana that I can introduce this technique to little kids whom I am training from the age group of ten to fifteen years: to improve concentration, to inculcate some kind of belief in their own ability and some kind of discipline which cricket requires for the betterment of their own personality and for the betterment of society in which they are going to grow up. And also if I may say so, to eliminate the possibility of ball tampering, betting and bribery. I am sure, this technique would help to a great extent.

Mr Bishen Singh Bedi
Sportsman, Delhi

We have to try ourselves, the Buddha cannot enlighten us. For this Vipassana is one of the ways.

We should try to introduce Vipassana into government schools for the primary age group if possible, and certainly at the upper secondary level. Vipassana is important, not only for the way of life but to give a real direction which is needed by students today.

Venerable Dhammaviriyo
National Minorities Commission
Delhi

I have prepared a few comments on Dharma and politics.

Politics is the theory and practice of government, of power. In the old days the sphere of power was limited and it was used for limited purposes. There have been various forms of government: monarchy, dictatorship and so on. The aim of government was administration, by and large for the good of the people, and so administrators were expected to be benevolent. A benevolent government or dictator was the cherished ideal of the society. They were expected to be religious, well-meaning. When the rulers were selfish and cruel, the sufferings of humanity were horrifying.

In modern times the sphere of political power has become almost all-pervading. There has been more and more dependence on and concentration of power. The concept of the welfare state has been demanding much more from governments, politicians and administrators. Compared to the past, this power needs to be used more judiciously, for the good of all the members of the human society. Towards that end many ideas, constitutional provisions, rules, regulations, checks and balances have been provided. New forms of government have been evolved. The latest form is the democratic way of government which has been defined as government of the people, for the people and by the people. Yet, the supreme guarantee of the benevolent, dutiful, honest and humane behaviour of these politicians is their inner goodness and consciousness.

Herein lies the role of Dharma, the Dharma that teaches the basic concepts of humane behaviour, concern for the human values of love, respect and affection for everybody, co-operation, acceptance and coexistence. In my view the political system must have a sound base of Dharma, by which I mean the human religion. However what is being said and practised in the name of religion today often reflects widespread misunderstanding and misuse. If we look at the basic or fundamental tenets of all religions, they are more or less the same: truth, love, respect, concern for the poor, concern for needy and suffering human beings. Yet battles, brutalities, killings and discrimination inflicted upon the human race has been in the name of religion. Therefore when we talk of religion, we should be clear that it is not any of the organised group of religions that we are talking about but the fundamentals of the human religion that needs to be accepted and introduced in human behaviour in general and among the politicians in particular. This may provide some solution to our present problems.

What is necessary is to bring about change and improvement in the individual attitude and the attitude of the society. There are many ways to bring about this change and one of them is the practice of Vipassana. I have during my life been practising *Svādhyāya*, the Yoga sutras but recently I came in contact with Goenkaji and I had the good fortune to undergo several courses. On the basis of personal experience, I have come to the conclusion that the greatest and the most important way of changing the behavioral pattern of the human being is through Vipassana. Therefore I feel that the introduction of religion in the field of politics (not in the form of organised religion as such, but in the form of Dharma) is most essential and that alone will save humanity from politics and its excesses.

Mr Madhukarrao Chaudhary
Former Speaker, Legislative Assembly
Mumbai

Over the last few years many of India's neighbours have achieved great increases in per capita Gross National Product, but India is lagging behind.

In a recent discussion I was told that the Japanese are so hard-working that we cannot hope to compete with them. But I maintain that one Indian is worth two Japanese. However, two Indians are worth one Japanese, and three Indians are worth zero! We don't know how to work together, we are always pulling in opposite directions.

Since 1991 the Government has ushered in an era of free market economy; protection is gone, and we are now part of a global system. Our success depends on quality, competitiveness and reliability, and so we must establish more efficient systems. If we do this, we have the potential soon to enjoy great prosperity.

If we want to be efficient in our work, sharp and discriminating intelligence is required, as well as loving relations with each other. Efficiency without love becomes a breeding ground for quarrels and strife. This is where applying the principles of Dharma can help.

Vipassana aims at establishing the practitioner in Dharma through insight meditation. The Buddha described the fruits of Dharma as *maitri* (loving-kindness), *karuṇā* (compassion), *muditā* (joy) and *upekṣā* (equanimity). These are obtained through the path of *sīla, samādhi* and *paññā*.

I do not believe there is any contradiction in terms when talking about Vipassana, an integral part of Dharma, together with economic gains. Wealth is not a bad word in the Indian psyche, it is very much a part of our thought process, as a means to an end of doing something good.

All who believe in eliminating poverty and bringing in prosperity will agree that we should aim at improving the productivity of our farms and factories, to produce things of higher quality at lower costs and achieve competitiveness in foreign markets.

Certainly, to gratify the senses is not the prime necessity or aim of a civilised mind. That only wealth brings happiness is an illusion. Dharma detaches us from such ignorance and enjoins us to eliminate suffering. We can take the help of modern science and technologies, guidance on principles of management, their know-how and so on.

Vipassana, which is our own inheritance, will help us to achieve our ultimate aims; it will help us to lift ourselves, not only spiritually but also materially.

Dr. Mohan Patel
Former Sheriff of Mumbai

My name is Kalburgi Srinivas. I am a professor at the University of Regina in Canada. I am now a foreigner in this country, where I was born and raised. India is a country where for centuries foreigners have come for its gold or golden ideas and thoughts. I too am such a foreigner now, who has come to collect golden ideas, noble thoughts for improving management and for transformation of organisations.

In this present environment, which is very complex, turbulent and competitive, and creates a lot of anxiety in organisations, you may say, "Why would anyone want to come to India to learn about management unless he wants to learn about the corruption, and organised gang management in Mumbai? This was a subject raised yesterday by Mr Khairnar." At other levels, those of you who have tried to get a telephone connection or get LPG gas or have chanced to go to a court of law, obtain a train ticket or even to seek admission for your child to school will have experienced a lot of frustrations. So that is the management system we have in this country.

Then what am I doing here? There are four premier schools of management in India, Indian Institutes of Management. I have been to all of them. I could not find anything "Indian" about them—maybe because they feel that India has nothing to teach in terms of management.

While Indian organisations and Indians as a whole are not known for their task accomplishment, the Indians who have gone abroad are all hard-working, creative, intelligent, entrepreneurial, and highly successful—so much so today, the ethnic community that is most affluent in the United States is our community, the South Asian community. So what is the problem? The problem does not appear to be in the genes that are in the South Asians.

Recently, however, practising managers in India have taken to making indigenous experiments to "Indianise" their management. Not Indian professors, but Indian managers. Some of them have been tremendously successful in economic terms. And this is the India I came to study.

For the past five months it has taken me from one uplifting, from one up-ending, from one pleasing experience to another.

I studied various spiritual movements and was impressed with their work. These techniques have been helping many executives and managers to look inward, to look inside themselves. Some remarkable changes are taking place in some of the organisations following this value-based management. I have also seen some eclectic experiments.

Now I have discovered Vipassana. It's a powerful technique to bring about transformational change in persons and through persons, in organisations. At least three organisations I have visited incorporate the technique in their way of working.

So there are many positive examples that we can be proud about which I'll be taking back with me. I'm not denying the existence of the India that Mr. Khairnar described yesterday, but that degraded India exists more because of the silence of good people like us. Let's recall the Gandhian movement which succeeded only because more and more people stood up to the authorities. They had to pay a price, yes, they paid it, and we may also have to pay a price to bring about dharmic rājya again. I have a few more comments but I am pleased about the fact that I was here, that I have been here, and what I have seen. And rest assured that I'll be back again in order to experience myself, going deeper into myself because I still have to learn a lot of things about myself.

Professor Kalburgi Srinivas
Canada

Let me make some suggestions based on my involvement with work organisations. One plea for action is to develop new dharma-based organisations. This means that we need to translate the four good qualities about which the Buddha spoke—compassion, loving-kindness, sympathetic joy and equanimity—to the workings of organisations themselves. "Sympathetic joy" has recently reappeared in organisations in an interesting way. This has come about through the Japanese influence and it is now quite common in India to talk not of satisfaction but of delight, not only amongst customers but also amongst employees. Many organisations in India are now measuring their effectiveness not only by financial results, important though these are. Profits are not now the direct concern of top management; they are more concerned about how to create delight for customers and high satisfaction for their employees. They realise that if these matters are attended to, then the financial results will follow.

In organisations, we need to pay attention to at least three aspects: the structure, the processes and the practices operating within each organisation. For instance, most organisations today, especially newly created ones, must pay attention to ecology, how the campus is created. Dharma-based organisations must examine their physical structure, which should reflect some of the values shown in the Dharma. The campus itself should be inspiring and should indicate and thus communicate the kind of values the organisation has.

Then there is the organisational structure itself. So if, for example, we have *mettā* as the basic foundation then the structure must be non-hierarchical. By contrast, if the organisation is deeply hierarchical, it will be difficult to practise the principles of loving-kindness. Most organizations today are concerned about this sense of equality and togetherness, and pressure is coming from another angle (again the Japanese influence) but I think the Indian experience has shown that it is possible to have non-hierarchical organisations and still get results.

Then, as far as organisational procedures are concerned, there are exemplary things happening in India, where organisations are adopting the traditional Dharma way of decision-making. For instance, in one well-known industrial company the main decision-making council consists of people from all parts of the enterprise, including the workers having the longest service, also the best workers, as well as the managers. The decisions made by this council are binding on the management, so they cannot ignore it.

I would recommend a book by Silvera titled *Human Resource Development—the Indian Experience,* in which he cites many examples of how Indian values are being inculcated in organisations.

Then when we look at the personnel practices in organisations we should examine whether such practices accord with the principles of Dharma and what new practices may need to be evolved. In the Human Resource Development Academy, which is a voluntary non-profit organization, we are already examining the kinds of values depicted, and I think for the future we might also include a Dharma perspective so that we can communicate what kind of values the various practices reflect. For if practices are based on those values which we wish to inculcate, we will have value-based organisations rather than the belief, or the myth, that management can be value-free. Serious analysis and conscious commitments are required to establish and maintain such value-based, Dharma organisational practices.

The individual should be at the centre of all these deliberations. Vipassana has a particular role here as one of the ways of helping people to examine themselves, based on experience, which is more important than the knowledge we receive from others. However public talks and seminars in which people share perspectives can also play their part. Positive experiences generate positivity. Then there is the service orientation, doing something good for humanity and the wider society. These values should be inculcated not by preaching but by ensuring that they are pragmatic in nature and assist the organisation to achieve its goals.

Finally there is the role of the guide or "mentor" as modern management describes it. Those who have been initiated in Vipassana, for example, and have developed in wisdom, not necessarily those holding hierarchical positions, can become informal leaders in the organisation: they can support others to gain strength in Dhamma—young people, for instance, who may be very bright but at the same time vulnerable.

An experienced and respected mentor can do much to inculcate values in a way that cannot be achieved by more formal means. Let us also then develop the role of mentors in our organisations to provide the necessary guidance and inspiration.

Professor Udai Pareek
Jaipur

Dharma and Science

Prof. P.L. Dhar

Inquisitiveness is one of the fundamental characteristics of human beings. Right from birth, a child would like to know and understand the surrounding world. As the child grows up, he or she begins to understand the cause-effect relationship between various events: putting a switch down lights a bulb, putting an ice cube in a glass of soft drink cools it, placing a hand in fire heats it—and we say, the child is learning, gaining knowledge. Science is essentially a systematisation of all the knowledge that humanity has gained about the external world, with the help of our senses.

As the child grows into maturity and experiences the various vicissitudes of life, sooner or later, he or she begins to question: "What is the purpose of all this—being born, studying, earning, having children, rearing a family, getting old and finally dying? Why so much suffering—caused by illness, old age, separation from loved ones, association with the 'wicked'?" He begins to contemplate and understand his own true nature, the real cause of his suffering, and the way out of it, and thus becomes wiser. Dharma is essentially a systematisation of all the wisdom gained by humanity.

Viewed in this way, Dharma and science emerge as two complementary aspects of human endeavour. As the Isa-Upanishad puts it, "He who has both spiritual wisdom (Dharma) and secular knowledge (science) together keeps death at bay through the latter and experiences immortality through the former."[1]

Science (especially its applied version, technology), gives us the necessary know-how to keep our body in good shape; Dharma provides us with an understanding of the very purpose of our existence, the "know-where". Clearly, for the harmonious development of any society—for the harmonious development of any individual—a proper integration of science and Dharma is essential. This is especially crucial in modern times, when the advances in science and technology have empowered us enormously. However, from a lack of "wisdom", of Dharma, this advancement in science is leading only to an increase in our sorrows: poisoning of land, air, water and of minds.

Misunderstandings about Dharma

The term "Dharma" literally means "natural law". Dharma is thus an exposition of the laws pertaining to our inner world, just as science deals with the laws pertaining to the outer world. The difference between science and Dharma is thus only a difference in the realm of enquiry—as there are differences between the various "departments" of science, such as physics, chemistry and botany. Yet there is a perception of irreconcilability between science and Dharma.

Many factors are responsible for this perception, the first and foremost being the erroneous understanding of both Dharma and science. Today, for most people, Dharma is synonymous with sectarian religions, with priestcraft; they see it as a mumbo-jumbo of words and elaborate rites and rituals, which can become the cause of internecine conflicts between neighbours, even though they may have lived like brothers for generations. Above all, Dharma has become synonymous with a stubborn resistance to any logical scrutiny of religious beliefs. No wonder the youth of today do not want to touch it with a barge-pole! A modern, rational person who is not willing to accept anything on authority—be it the authority of a religious teacher or a sacred book—is therefore tempted to reject it all often, even the eternal truths which are so badly needed to give direction to life will be rejected, thus throwing the baby out with the bath-water! This process is catalysed by a scientific temperament, which is equated with crass materialism—for hasn't science got an explanation for every phenomenon on the basis of matter in motion under the influence of various forces? Therefore, anyone talking about the existence of reality beyond sensory perception is usually dubbed as unscientific—an ignorant fool living in a world of his own fancies. In such a scenario, the integration of science and Dharma is obviously impossible.

To change this situation there is clearly a need to present Dharma as a science, following a scientific method, shorn of all extraneous socio-political adjuncts and metaphysical speculations. The scientific attitude demands "induction from facts and not deduction from dogmas. We must face the facts and derive our conclusion from them and not start with the conclusion and then play with the facts."[2] Secondly, we also need to understand whether materialism, a legacy of nineteenth-century science, is still endorsed by modern science. Fortunately, recent developments in science are questioning this traditional world view, and thus a proper understanding of these developments can give a fillip to the process of integrating science and Dharma.

Dharma as an Applied Science

The essence of the scientific approach was characterised by Thomson: "The aim of science is to describe impersonal facts of experience in verifiable terms as exactly as possible, as simply as possible, and as completely as possible."[3]

To become a rigorous science, Dharma must be presented as "the Law" which can be experienced by all, not merely a select few. The various propositions have to be presented as hypotheses to be accepted only on verification by experience, albeit personal and subjective,* and not on authority. Also, such propositions should be rational and logical.

The teachings of the Buddha, one of the greatest spiritual scientists, meet these requirements. His constant refrain to his disciples could easily be the advice of a modern humane scientist to young students:

> Believe nothing merely because you have been told it, or because it is tradition, or because you yourself have imagined it. Do not believe what your teacher tells you merely out of respect for him. But whatever, after due examination and analysis, you find to be conducive to the good, the benefit, the welfare of all beings,

* Given the nature of enquiry, spiritual experience is personal; but it is not a private fact. It is predictable and verifiable in the personal experience of others.[6]

believe and cling to that doctrine, and take it as your guide.

The essence of Dharma, as put crisply by all the Enlightened Ones is "the eschewing of all evil, the perfecting of good deeds, the purifying of one's mind."[4]

The simplicity of this enunciation, devoid of any esoteric pronouncement, may sometimes conceal its profundity. However, its practical utility and universal applicability are quite obvious. Viewed in this light, purifying the mind of its baser instincts is the quintessence of Dharma, since this would quite naturally lead to performance of wholesome deeds. It also leads to the development of an insight into the basic characteristics of life. This process of purification is not a mystic knowledge beyond the ken of ordinary people. It is a strictly scientific technique open to anybody who is willing to learn and verify it.

Vipassana—the Quintessence of Dharma

The process of purification of mind is analogous to cleaning the turbid waters of a lake. Two approaches are possible. One could use an external precipitating agent such as alum that chemically forces all the impurities to settle down at the bottom of the lake. Alternatively, one could go inside the lake, identify each and every impurity, and actually take it out. Clearly, the latter process is bound to be more messy and will need more effort, but its advantages are quite obvious. With the former method, we are only suppressing the impurities, but they are still very much there at the bottom. A major storm or churning of the lake can bring them to the surface again. However, with the latter method we have actually eliminated them and the lake will remain clean, so long as we do not add fresh impurities to it. The ancient masters recognised both these approaches, that is to say either suppression or elimination of the mental defilements.

If we divert our attention away from the defilements* as and when they arise (for example by listening to music, or having a drink, or chanting a "holy" name, or some lofty auto-suggestion) the intensity of these negative emotions abates quickly and we can get immediate relief. However these defilements are not actually eradicated, but only suppressed. Modern psychology agrees that they leave their impressions in the deeper recesses of the mind, in its subconscious and unconscious layers.

To remove the impurities of the mind, it is obviously necessary to identify them objectively, and it turns out that this detached "observation" of the mental-physical structure is sufficient to eliminate them. An incident from life of Swami Vivekananda illustrates this point. Once, as he was walking on a street in Varanasi, some monkeys started chasing him. At first Swamiji tried to run from them, but the monkeys kept pace and began to attack him. Just then an old man called out, "Face the brutes." Swamiji turned and confronted the monkeys, and when he did they all fell back and fled.

The impurities of the mind are like these monkeys and the only way to eradicate them is to face them squarely—to observe them without reacting. But how are we to observe these defilements? How does one observe anger, for example, without actually getting overwhelmed by it?

---

* such as anger, hatred, vengefulness, despair, regret, arrogance, greed, envy, lust, pride, etc.

The ancient masters who unravelled the complexities of body-mind phenomena with penetrating insight discovered an imprortant fact: "Whatever arises in the mind is accompanied by sensation" *(sabbe dhammā vedanā samosaraṇā).*[5] They also found that all our reactions to various situations are in reality the reactions of the subconscious mind to bodily sensations. Now, while it is very difficult to observe objectively abstract emotions such as anger or passion, it is comparatively easy to train the mind to observe sensations (which carry the signatures of these emotions) in a detached manner. The continuous practice of observing these bodily sensations objectively is the crux of Vipassana meditation. Slowly, but surely, it grinds out the deep mental grooves of lifelong habits—craving for pleasant experiences, avoiding the unpleasant, and ignoring neutral experiences. It thus gradually lifts the veil which obscures from us the real characteristics of all body-mind phenomena: impermanence, unsatisfactoriness and egolessness.

To be able to observe the sensations which keep on occurring continuously in various parts of the body, a minimum level of concentration of the mind is obviously essential so that one does not get easily distracted by the external and inner noises which are the hallmarks of our modern life.

The training of increasing the concentration of mind can be done in a variety of ways. In Vipassana, the object of concentration is one's own breath. This practice is called Anapana, which literally means incoming and outgoing breath. It involves bare observation of the normal, natural respiration with a firm and steady attention, free from any strain. Again, there is no mystery about the choice of breath as the object of concentration; there are many sound reasons for it. Firstly, breath is universally acceptable, being non-sectarian. Also, it is readily available at any time and it is a neutral object: no-one has any craving or aversion towards it. Focusing attention on such an object continuously for a long period of time is, of course, quite difficult, given our present disposition, which only seeks excitement through pleasant objects. But a systematic, persistent effort does make a dent in this stubborn habit.

As a result we receive a foretaste of the fruits of equableness—a natural feeling of peace and tranquillity accompanying the sharpening of the mind. One could have chosen an object of concentration for which the meditator has some attraction or reverence. This would have made the task of concentration much easier because of the natural attraction for the object, but, as is obvious, this would only strengthen the mental habit of craving and thus take us away from the goal of complete purification of mind.

An obvious prerequisite for such a training is the scrupulous observance of basic moral precepts—in particular, abstention from killing, stealing, false speech, sexual misconduct, and intoxicants—since their wilful violation would cause violent mental agitation, making it impossible to observe the mind-body complex objectively. Vipassana practitioners can thus learn by experience the importance of moral conduct for their own well-being. In this way morality and ethics thus become a scientific discipline, which one accepts on the basis of one's own experience and not on account of social pressures or respect for a teacher. This was the fond wish of Albert Einstein, one of the greatest scientists of all times: "The foundation of morality should not be made dependent on myth nor tied to any authority lest doubts about the myth or about the legitimacy of the authority imperil the foundation of sound judgement and action."

From the above description of the basic features of Vipassana, it is apparent that it is an applied science, a technology for inner development. In the true scientific spirit, all that it involves is mindful observation, free from any admixture of prejudices or subjective judgements. Like any other modern technology, it has a scientific basis which can be easily understood; and what is more important, its results can easily be verified by personal experience, here and now. *Ehi passiko, ehi passiko* (come and see, come and see) was the constant refrain of the Buddha. There is no rite or ritual, dogma or *a priori* belief necessary for the meditation. Like any other technological skill it can be learnt by systematic practice irrespective of one's caste, creed, religious belief or nationality.

Though its most important objective is to purify the mind of dross, Vipassana is not a mere detergent to wash the dirt off the mental linens, and then to be left behind in the washroom after use. It is an attitude to life, a fragrance which naturally envelops practitioners as they develop more and more insight into the fundamental traits of human existence. It is an art of living equanimously in spite of defeats and victories, praise and criticism, falling health and rising prices. It is the art of transcending, and not suppressing, the sensory attractions. As the practice matures, one naturally develops a deep insight into the fundamental laws of life and becomes harmonious with these. One becomes established in Dharma.

Science and Materialism

It is historical fact that the rise of science in the post-Renaissance period was instrumental in spreading a general belief in materialism—a belief that matter is the sole reality. All the phenomena of nature, ranging from the motion of the planets to the tides in the seas, could now be explained rationally on the basis of well understood laws of nature. There was no need whatsoever for invoking divine intervention. Even the origin of sentient beings could be "explained" on the basis of the Darwinian theory of evolution.

Some people tried to further extend this theory to show that the simplest form of living protoplasm could arise from non-living nitrogenous carbon compounds under suitable conditions—thus exploding the age-old argument for the existence of God. Attempts were even made to explain consciousness and thinking as arising from the functions of the ganglionic cells of the cortex of the brain. The scientists of the last century firmly held that it should be possible to explain the universe with a few score elements and half a dozen elementary forces.[7] No wonder, for most people today, the scientific approach is synonymous with a belief in materialism, a belief in the omnipotence of intellect, and any suggestion about "transcending the intellect" is seen as unscientific.

This picture has, however, undergone considerable change in the last few decades. New developments in science such as the theory of relativity and quantum mechanics, are bringing about a profound change in our common-sense view of nature. Many illuminating books have been written in the last two decades which bring out the various facets of this emerging change. We shall mention here only a few of these points which seem most pertinent for our discussion.

Fundamental Nature of Matter

The quest for the basic building blocks of matter led scientists to what are often called fundamental particles: electrons, protons, neutrons etc. The intuitive model of the atom which emerges from this research is similar to the planetary system—with a heavy nucleus (consisting of neutrons and protons) at the centre of an immense void, and tiny electrons whirling round it at very high speeds. Naturally, at first these fundamental particles were thought to be something similar to the classical particles, albeit ultra-small—something like specks of dust often seen in the path of a ray of sunshine entering a room. Belief in this concept has, however, been badly shaken by many discoveries. Experimental studies showed that these particles they could be "created" out of energy and could "vanish" in energy as predicted by Einstein's theory of the interconvertibility of matter and energy.

Now, since energy is a dynamic quantity associated with activity or with processes, the obvious implication is that "a particle has to be conceived as a dynamic pattern, a process involving the energy which manifests itself as the particle's mass".[8] This is a picture which is in great contrast to our common-sense notion of "mass" as belonging to an object, but in consonance with the insight of ancient masters: "No doer is there; naught save the deed is... The path exists, but not the traveller found on it".[9]

It will probably take even the scientific community many more years to fully come to terms with the philosophical implications of Einstein's theory of relativity. Even today the import of Minkowski's oft-quoted enunciation: "Space by itself and time by itself are mere shadows of a four-dimensional space-time continuum which is an independent reality".[10] We do not understand because we have no direct sensory or even intuitive experience of this four-dimensional space-time continuum. Evidently our perception of the world based on the common-sense view of absolute space and time is in error. The situation is quite akin to the erroneous view of the prisoners of Plato's Republic, who never having seen anything other than the shadows on the walls of their underground cave, mistook these for reality.[10]

An experience of this independent reality would clearly demand transcendence of the senses, coming out of the "prison house of sight". This is a term which we find repeatedly in the ancient texts, but something which would have been anathema to the nineteenth-century scientist. As Fritjof Capra, quoting Swami Vivekananda, puts it, this space-time of relativistic physics is the Absolute of Eastern sages: "Time, space and causation are like the glass through which the absolute is seen. In the Absolute there is neither time, space nor causation."[11] This conception thus gives scientific authority (probably needed for the sceptics) to the vision of the ancient sages. Having experienced the transcendent reality directly, they declared: "There is, brethren, an unborn, a not-become, a not-made, not-compounded."[12]

Understanding "Reality"

Another mind-boggling characteristic of these fundamental particles, which has defied all conventional explanations is their ability to exhibit both "wave" and "particle" behaviour under certain experimental conditions.

The fundamental particles thus do not seem to possess any intrinsic nature waiting to be revealed to an inquisitive observer. As summed up by Capra:

> My conscious decision about how to observe, say, an electron will determine the electron's properties to some extent. If I ask it a particle question, it will give me a particle answer. If I ask it a wave question, it will give me a wave answer. The electron does not have objective properties independent of my mind.

We could thus say, with Sir James Jeans, that, in the light of this discovery,

> the universe begins to look more like a great thought than like a great machine. Mind no longer appears as an intruder into the realm of matter ... but ... as the creator and the governor of the realm of matter—not of course our individual mind, but the Mind in which the atoms, out of which our individual minds have grown, exist as thoughts.

Any further understanding of the nature of ultimate reality clearly demands an investigation into the subtle mental plane—self-analysis rather than analysis of the world around, thus merging Science with Dharma.

It is also evident from the above description that an intuitive physical model of these fundamental particles is not possible since our senses can only detect either particle motion, characterised by a localisation of the object moving in a definite trajectory in space, or a wave motion, characterised by a motion of the medium. This realisation forms the basis of one of the very important principles of quantum mechanics: the Principle of Complementarity put forth by Niels Bohr. That is, in any experiment with micro-particles, the observer gets information not about the "properties of the particles themselves", but about the properties of the particles associated with some particular situation. This includes, among other things, the measuring instruments. The information obtained under some definite conditions should be considered as complementary to the information obtained under different experimental conditions. Evidence obtained under experimental conditions cannot be comprehended within a single picture, but must be regarded as various sides (complementing each other) of a single reality—to wit, the object under investigation.[15]

The social and philosophical implications of this principle are profound. It gives credence to the insight of ancient masters that our attempts at understanding "reality" through the study of matter with the senses are similar to the attempts of five blind men trying to comprehend an elephant by feeling it with their hands. The evidence thus obtained can never be synthesized into the true picture. Clearly, it follows that to comprehend the "reality" of matter, it is necessary to use some other mode of gathering knowledge—*aparokṣānubhūti* or direct experience, as our ancient sages put it.

At the social level, this complementary principle points out that apparently contradictory views may emerge from the same "reality". Wisdom lies in treating them as complementary; this is a message of harmony needed so much in modern times when "appearances" often lead to unending conflicts. In fact Bohr fervently hoped that the complementary principle would, in the near future, find a place in school education.

A New World View

There have been many developments in other sciences such as biology, psychology, chemistry, neurosciences, etc. All of these indicate the emergence of a new world view which repudiates materialism, but is in consonance with the vision of the Eastern sages of yore. In fact many of the insights of these sages remained unintelligible to the masses, based as they were on the transcendent experience; but today they can be better appreciated in the light of these scientific facts.

One such fundamental insight, which is extremely difficult to comprehend on the basis of our common-sense view of nature, is that of *anattā*—the fact of egolessness. However, when modern science tells us that the basic building block of matter is not a "being" but a manifestation of energy, which is essentially a process of "becoming", this assertion seems to make sense. It is this seemingly solid physical body, "my body", which creates the stubborn illusion of individuality. Modern biologists point out that 98 per cent of the 10^{28} atoms of a typical human body are replaced annually from the atoms of the surroundings—the earth, the trees, the animals, in fact all living and non-living entities. It thus becomes evident that one cannot talk of individual entities localised in space and time; we are all partners in a biodance.[16] Walt Whitman's poetic insight—"Every atom belonging to me as good belongs to you" —is thus a scientific fact!

Molecular biology associates our individuality with the uniqueness of the genes. But here too it is the pattern of the genes which remains the same and not the *stuff* of the gene—the thousands of individual carbon, hydrogen, oxygen, and other atoms that comprise it, which are in constant exchange with the surroundings.[16] So, even in the view of hard-core molecular biology, our individuality is a non-material "entity", an abstract pattern of arrangement of various labile molecules. When we couple this understanding with the impossibility of "exactly" locating any fundamental particle, as revealed by Heisenberg's Uncertainty Principle, and also with the fundamental interconnectedness at quantum level, one is forced to agree with Capra:

> The quantum field is seen as the fundamental physical entity; a continuous medium which is present everywhere in space. Particles are merely local condensations of the field; concentrations which come and go, thereby losing their individual character and dissolving into the underlying field.

This quantum field is obviously an impersonal entity—the nearest symbol which one can possibly conceive of for the transcendent reality. As even a layman today would testify, a subset of this field—the electromagnetic field—does have the "power" to produce the splendid illusion of a "living being" in every home—on television! One can thus appreciate that the fundamental quantum field could be responsible for creating the illusion of the existence of the viewer of the television too. That this viewer is illusory is the insight of *anattā*!

Concluding Remarks

Both Dharma and Science enunciate the laws of nature; as applicable to the inner world of human beings and the external world. There can be no disharmony between them, for as Gary Zukav points out in his recent book,

> [The laws of Science] are the reflection in physical reality—in the world of physical objects and phenomena—of a larger non-physical dynamic at work in non-physical domains. When Science and its discoveries are understood with the

higher order of logic and understanding of the multisensory human,* they reveal the same richness that Life itself displays everywhere and endlessly... the paradigms... of Science also reveal the way our species has seen itself in relation to the Universe: Newtonian physics reflects a species that is confident in its ability to grasp the dynamics of the physical world through the intellect; relativity reflects a species that understands the limiting relationship between the absolute and the personalised conception of it; and quantum physics reflects a species that is becoming aware of the relationship of its consciousness to the physical world.[18]

It would thus not be an exaggeration to say that for a deeper understanding of modern science, there is a need to develop certain intuitive insights. These can enable us to have experiences more rich than those possible with the basic five senses. Clearly, the process of evolution of such a *multisensory personality* can be hastened by living life in conformity with the Universal Laws, the Dharma—that is, by practising Vipassana.

The complementarity of science and Dharma can be succinctly put by paraphrasing the beautiful epigram of Albert Einstein: Science without Dharma is blind and Dharma without Science is lame—for Dharma gives us the vision of what ought to be done, and Science gives us the power to do it[19]. The developments in science have unleashed enormous power—but power can do as much harm as good. Today, there is a crying need to channel this power to ensure the very survival of humanity, for otherwise Man will destroy himself by misusing the same power. What we must do is reorient our lives in the light of the quintessence of Dharma, by practising morality *(sīla)*, taming the senses by the practice of concentration *(samādhi)* and progressively purifying the mind by the practice of Vipassana.

* one whose perceptions extend beyond the sensory domain to the larger dynamic systems of which our physical reality is a part.

References

1. Dhar, P.L. and R.R. Gaur. Science and Humanism—Towards a Unified World View, Commonwealth publishers, New Delhi, 1992, p. 128.

2. Radhakrishnan,S. An Idealist View of Life, George Allen and Unwin (India), Bombay, 1976, p. 13.

3. Thomson, J.A. Introduction to Science, Henry Holt & Company, New York, 1911.

4. Radhakrishnan, S. The Dhammapada, Oxford University Press, London, 1950, verse 183.

5. Hart, William The Art of Living, Vipassana Research Institute, Igatpuri, 1993, p. 148.

6. Budhananda, Swami Can One be Scientific and yet Spiritual?, Advaita Ashram, Calcutta,1976, p. 43.

7. Nirvedananda, Swami Religion and Modern Doubts, Ramakrishna Mission, Calcutta, 1979, p. 27.

8. Dhar, P.L. and R.R. Gaur, op. cit., p. 77.

9. Warren, H. C. Buddhism in Translations, Motilal Banarasi Das Publishers, New Delhi, 1986, p. 146.

10. Minkowski, H., quoted in Rydnik, V., ABC of Quantum Mechanics, Mir Publishers, Moscow, 1965, p. 175.

11. Capra, F. The Tao of Physics, Fontana, Collins, 1976, p. 186.

12. Ranganathananda, Swami Eternal Values for a Changing Society, Vol. 2, Bhartiya Vidya Bhavan, 1987.

13. Capra, F., op. cit. p. 77.

14. Jeans, James quoted in Nirvedanada, Swami, op cit., p. 37

15. Neils Bohr quoted in Tarasov, L.V., Basic Concepts of Quantum Mechanics, Mir Publishers, Moscow, 1980, p. 152.

16. Dossey, L. Space, Time and Medicine, Shambhala Publications, 1982, p. 72-73.

17. Capra, F., quoted in above, p. 80.

18. Zukav, G. The Seat of the Soul, Rider, London, 1990, p. 67.

19. Einstein, A. quoted in Budhananda, S., Can One be Scientific and yet Spiritual, Advaita Ashram, Calcutta, 1976, p. 31.

Discussion Extracts

I will give just one example of how science without Dharma is blind.

Many years ago there was a tragedy in Bhopal. I was a witness to that. I live in Bhopal. The Union Carbide plant emitted huge amounts of highly toxic gas. They didn't know what effects it would produce. It killed thousands of people that very day. It affected about 500,000 people in the city. People continued to die, I think by now the dead number between 10,000 and 15,000. People are still suffering to this day.

Whatever science knew was done. Hundreds of doctors and the Indian Council of Medical Research, in all its strength, came and provided the best services at their disposal. The social scientists were also there trying to see what they could do.

As a consequence of this, several hundred crores of rupees were spent and assistance given: hospitals, dispensaries and various centres were opened. But the end result was—I observed it all at close quarters—nothing really changed.

People got money; they gambled with that money or spent it on liquor, and the crime rate increased. When science had gone ahead with its research to produce that gas, it had not discovered the full facts about the gas, about the consequences if a leak occurred. The doctors then did not know and disputes continue till now about the correct method of dealing with this tragedy. This, then, is what happens if science goes unbridled without Dharma.

Mr. M.S. Choudhary
Former Chief Secretary
Madhya Pradesh

Professor Dhar gave a very lucid exposition of how the Buddha was a scientist. From what I have read in the texts and commentarial literature, it has become clear to me that indeed he was a real scientist. Whatever he said about mind can only be said by a scientist, a psychologist of great depth.

Our mind, he said, keeps jumping like a monkey from one object to another. This is exactly what we experience when we sit in a Vipassana course and try to look within. We soon come to the realisation that the mind is difficult to control, fickle and unsteady. In order to control mind Buddha prescribed different subjects of meditation for different types of persons. The monasteries were actually the laboratories and workshops for the process of purification of mind.

Again the Buddha was really a scientist in the sense that he discovered some laws operating within ourselves, not only in the outside world. The laws that he discovered are eternal dhammas. Enmity cannot be appeased by enmity *(nāhi verena verāni samantidha kudācana),* it can be appeased only by non-enmity *(averena samantidha)*—this is eternal law *(esa dhammo sanantano).* Just like a scientist he made experiments and theorised only on the basis of his own experience. One finds evidence of this repeatedly in the Dhammapada and the Tipiṭaka in general. By going beyond the realm of reason, by developing non-attachment to the changing nature of mind and body, he attained *nibbāna* and became a Buddha—a fully enlightened person.

Dr. Angaraj Chaudhary
(Retired Professor of Pāli
Nava Nālandā Mahāvihāra)
VRI, Igatpuri

Vipassana—A Practical Solution

Ian Hetherington

Suppose we accept that Dharma or Dhamma, a universal law of nature, exists. Simply by observing the world around us—night and day, the seasons, the cycle of birth, life and death affecting all living beings—we are aware of this law. Scientists probe to discover still more abstract patterns in the universe. We might also concede that *karma* or *kamma*, the law of cause and effect, fuelled by our actions of body, speech and mind, is equally timeless and real when applied to human behaviour. We may accept these propositions at the emotional, devotional or intellectual level because they accord with our pre-existing view of the world. This is of limited practical use, however, because it cannot free us from the hatred, fear, anger, passion and other impurities stored in the depths of the mind, which continually overpower us in everyday life. Some way of obtaining direct access to Dharma, the law working within and without us, is required. For liberation, for lasting happiness, we need to develop wisdom based on personal experience of our own internal reality. Vipassana is a technique for this purpose.

What Vipassana Is

Vipassana meditation is a method of self-observation. In the ancient language of India, *passanā* meant to look, to see with open eyes, in the ordinary way. But *vipassanā* is to observe things as they really are, not merely as they seem to be. Apparent truth has to be penetrated until one reaches the ultimate truth of the entire mental and physical structure. It is a logical process of mental purification leading gradually towards full enlightenment. Vipassana meditation is the essence of what the Buddha practised and taught. It is a straightforward, practical way to achieve peace of mind and to live a happy, useful life. The meditation does not encourage people to withdraw from society, rather it strengthens them to face all the ups and downs of life in a calm and balanced way. The approach can be summarized in a few short lines:

To abstain from evil,
To do good,
To purify the mind.

Simple objectives but so difficult to practise.

Learning the Technique

To learn Vipassana it is necessary to take a ten-day residential course under the guidance of a qualified teacher. During the retreat students remain within the course site, having no contact with the outside world. Reading, writing and all religious practices are suspended.

Students follow a demanding daily schedule, which includes about ten hours of sitting meditation. They also observe silence, not communicating with fellow students; however, they are free to discuss meditation questions with the teacher and material problems with the management.

The day begins at 4:30 AM with students meditating in their rooms or in the hall, where a chanting tape is played. Breakfast is served at 6:30, followed by group meditation in the hall and instructions from the teacher. Individual meditation then continues and the teacher checks students on their progress. Old students (meditators who have completed at least one Vipassana course in this tradition, are allocated individual cells to enable them to work more independently and seriously. Lunch is taken at 11:00; simple, nutritious, vegetarian food is served. A two-hour break in the middle of the day gives meditators an opportunity to rest, do their washing or exercise outside. The teacher is available for individual student interviews at this time. Meditation and checking continue in the afternoon. Tea and fruit for new students and lemon water for old students are served at 5:00. After the final session of group meditation, a taped evening discourse by S.N. Goenka clarifies each day's practice. The teacher is again available after the discourse to answer questions and students retire to bed by 9:30.

There is no charge whatsoever for the teaching. Costs are met by the donations of grateful students of past courses who have experienced the benefits of Vipassana, and who wish to give others the same unique opportunity. Neither the teacher nor the assistant teachers (over 250 appointed to date) receive remuneration; they and those who serve the courses volunteer their time.

Training the Mind

To learn Vipassana, there are three steps to the training.

First, students practise abstaining from actions which cause harm. They undertake five moral precepts: practising abstention from killing, stealing, sexual misconduct, wrong speech and the use of intoxicants. Following these precepts allows the mind to calm down sufficiently to proceed further.

Second, for the first three-and-a-half-days, students practise Anapana meditation, focusing attention on the breath. This practice helps to develop control over the unruly mind.

These first two steps—of living a wholesome life and developing control of the mind—are necessary and very beneficial. But they are incomplete unless the third step is taken: purifying the mind of underlying negativities. This step occupies the last six and a half days of the course. It is undertaken by the practice of Vipassana: one penetrates one's entire physical and mental structure with the clarity of insight.

Complete silence is observed for the first nine days. On the tenth day, students resume speaking, making the transition back to a more extroverted way of life.

The course finishes on the morning of the eleventh day. The retreat closes with the practice of *mettā-bhāvanā* (loving-kindness or goodwill to all), in which the purity developed during the course is shared with all beings.

Although Vipassana has been preserved in the Buddhist tradition, it contains nothing of a sectarian nature, and can be accepted and applied by people of any background. Courses are open to anyone sincerely wishing to learn the technique, irrespective of race, caste, faith or nationality. Hindus, Jains, Muslims, Sikhs, Buddhists, Christians, Jews as well as members of other religions have all successfully practised Vipassana.

Many leading members of religious groups have learned the technique and courses have been organized in traditional places of worship.

Vipassana in Everyday Life

Having taken a ten-day course the meditator is his or her own master. There is no gurudom in Vipassana. Equipped with an outline of the technique, the lay meditator faces the challenge of maintaining a daily practice and applying Dharma in everyday life, alongside routine work and family responsibilities. With strong determination initial difficulties will be overcome. Weekly sittings with other local meditators, giving service at a centre, or taking a weekend short course are just some of the very practical ways in which one can support and strengthen one's practice. With continuity of practice the meditator will assuredly taste the fruits of success, enabling him or her to become firmly established in Dharma.

Students are encouraged to evaluate their own progress on the path using various criteria, such as:

* Instead of hurting others, have I started helping them?
* How am I behaving in unwanted situations—am I reacting as before, with the same intensity of agitation and for the same length of time, or am I remaining more balanced?
* Am I becoming less self-centred, giving generously without expectation of anything in return, showing compassion to the needy, developing gratitude towards those who help me?
* Am I establishing my meditation on a sound foundation by keeping the five moral precepts in daily life?

From the beginning meditators are encouraged to become self-dependent in their practice. It is emphasized that whilst enlightened devotion to gods or saintly persons is helpful on the path if one tries to develop these same good qualities in oneself, liberation from mental impurity is the individual's responsibility. One has to work out one's own salvation and not look to external agencies to act on one's behalf.

A Technique for All

The Buddha's address to the people of the devoted Kalama clan in northern India twenty-five centuries back is justly famous:

> Do not simply believe any teaching you have heard. When you know for yourselves these things are unwholesome ... then reject them. But whenever you know for yourselves that something is conducive to welfare and happiness ... then accept it and live up to it.

His purpose was clear—to invite all who sincerely wish to learn to make their own free, objective enquiry into the nature of truth.

Any average person can learn, practise and benefit from Vipassana. But one has to work intelligently, ensuring that awareness and equanimity develop in equal measure. Most people have some appreciation of their own strengths and weaknesses. But this knowledge alone can lead to frustration, apathy or even despair. How can I change? How can I be free of the tendency to act wrongly, despite the best of intentions? Vipassana provides hope, strength and a practical tool for the realization of every individual. With practice, this process of observation of breath and body sensations produces wonderful results in everyday life.

To take a contemporary parallel: many nations, concerned about security, have invested in some kind of early warning system in case of attack by a foreign power. The Vipassana meditator soon learns that it is the enemy within oneself that requires maximum vigilance. And this same technique helps us to develop our own internal early warning system, to counter the old habit of blind reaction. Through the practice, we are taking proper preventive measures which are in our own and others' interest, rather than casting about for some remedy when the damage has already been done.

The Spread of Dharma

No-one should have any doubt about the non-sectarian nature of the technique. In teaching Vipassana the Buddha had no intention of establishing a sect or starting a personality cult. Those who practise are tasting the essence of pure Dharma; they are not getting converted into another religion. The objects of meditation in Vipassana, the natural breath and actual bodily sensations, are deliberately neutral. Similarly the complementary training in morality, mastery of mind and the development of insight should be acceptable to all genuine seekers after truth. The malady is universal, therefore the remedy likewise has to be universal. People from all backgrounds who practise Vipassana find that they become better human beings. If leading figures in the fields of religion, politics, economics, the professions, the arts, industry and business realise the potential for change which this technique offers, and use their influence wisely, much can be done to improve the level of harmony and well-being in Indian society and elsewhere.

Vipassana is one of India's most ancient meditation techniques, but over the centuries it became lost to the country. Fortunately the theory and practice were preserved in their purity by a chain of devoted teachers in neighbouring Myanmar (Burma). Through uninterrupted transmission, from generation to generation. This is how, by good fortune, we come to receive a technique as fresh and effective today as it was in the Buddha's time. Vipassana was re-introduced to the land of its origin in 1969 by Mr S.N. Goenka, a disciple of the respected Burmese lay meditation master, Sayagyi U Ba Khin. Since then people from all walks of life and many nationalities have benefited in growing numbers from participating in courses. Some thirty centres now exist worldwide for the exclusive teaching of this technique.

May pure Dharma continue to spread for the good and benefit of all beings.

Discussion Extracts

A search is on all over the world, by scientist engaged in the study of the human mind and its behaviour patterns, to find a method which can purify and transform mind. The key to the solution of all problems that affect human society lies in the discovery of this method.

Much of the trouble and tension result from rigid, fixed habit patterns. Every day we come across people apparently looking wise, intelligent and learned but deeply suffering because they cannot change their habits and behaviour patterns.

Another evil which has caused so much suffering in the lie of the individual is the human 'ego', a totally misplaced belief in the so-called 'I', 'me', 'mine', a created image so distorted and false, the cause of deep suffering. Similarly, 'my views', 'my opinion', 'my belief', 'my philosophy' become fetters and chains causing endless anguish.

Human history is replete with examples of how this 'ego' at the individual, group or even national level has been the cause of conflicts, wars, tension and turmoil. Justifiably, therefore, there is intense search for the solution.

Based on my own experience and the experience of thousands of people in India and in other countries who have gone through the training, it can be stated that Vipassana provides a solution, a method which brings purity of mind. No miracles are promised: ardous work is required for the process of self-improvement. However, the destination is sure: peace, harmony and happiness. It is worth giving a trial.

Mr Ram Singh, I.A.S. (Ret'd)
Jaipur

I am grateful for this opportunity to speak. My name is Dr Om Prakash, I am 83 years old, and have been practising medicine for the last 56 years. I am also a small-time Dhamma worker: I meditate, and on occasions talk about Dhamma.

Vipassana helps a lot in the practice of medicine. I was quite young when I started practising Vipassana. At that time I was staying in Myanmar (Burma) and had a flourishing practice, seeing 250 to 300 patients every day. On entering the clinic I used to be excited and agitated, wondering how I could see so many patients and how I could finish my work in time. I often used to lose my temper, would get angry at the nurse, and would shout at my assistant.

But as I started practising Vipassana I saw that I was able to work without losing my peace of mind. My medical practice grew, but I no longer felt agitated. My attitude towards my problems changed. Initially, I used to think about the patient's ability to pay for my treatment. After Vipassana, I started thinking: "Oh, what would I do if my son or grandson became sick. This child is like my grandson!" I found that now I had nothing but *karunā* (compassion) and *mettā* (loving-kindness) for my patients.

I also found that my treatments became more effective and beneficial. I was giving the same medicines, but the results were far better. The patients would become well more quickly, even though I was giving the same medicines! In fact, I was using smaller quantities, so people would ask if I was giving them homoeopathic medicines, and why I was not giving them modern allopathic medicines.

I realised that the medicines I gave were less important than my compassion and *mettā*. Patients started getting cured no matter what medicine I prescribed. Thus the professional can benefit from Vipassana and help people.

Secondly, I would like to talk about equanimity. I have written a small article in the Hindi Vipassana newsletter entitled "Let's Maintain Equanimity". One goes through many vicissitudes in life. My father passed away when I was 22, and I had six siblings. The responsibility of rearing them fell on my young shoulders. Somehow, I went through it.

Later during my medical career, I faced a difficult situation. The Burmese brothers sitting here know about it. The government of Myanmar had started an "Eagle Movement" at that time. Anybody could be arrested and put in jail without any reason being given. Family members would not even know where the person was imprisoned or how long it would be before he was released, if he was released at all.

One day some men came to my clinic and asked me to accompany them after seeing my patients. They were from the dreaded B.S.I., and a visit from them was like a death sentence at that time in Myanmar. I told my wife that I was going with these B.S.I. people and not to be afraid. I said, "I have done no wrong. I am clean. Do not bribe anybody. People will come saying that they have contacts with the B.S.I. or that they can get me out of prison, and they will demand money. Do not give any money, any bribe, however long I am held in prison. I am sure to come out some day."

It is hard for you to even imagine the jail conditions. The prison to which I was taken was built in 1908 by the British and is a very large prison like our Tihar Jail. I was kept in solitary confinement for thirty-five days. My room was about eight by ten feet in size and it also served as a latrine. Once in four days I would be taken out for a bath. Even that was a difficult affair. There was constant prodding from the warders to use less water and to be quick. A barber used to come once in about fifteen days. He would use a safety razor, but the shaving was more like grating, and the pain was beyond description, especially when he shaved the moustache area. Goenkaji describes many kinds of sensations during a Vipassana course, but this pain was so intense that it defies description.

But I can say with certainty that equanimity was maintained during the entire ordeal of thirty-five days. I was not at all worried. I continued my meditation. Finally, I was told that I was innocent and was allowed to go home. This was the effect of the equanimity of Vipassana.

Thanks to Vipassana, even at the age of 83, I can still stand on my own and talk, I am still active, I even see patients.

Dr Om Prakash
Vipassana Teacher and
Medical Practitioner, Delhi

I want to tell you about my experience of Vipassana. I came to Dhamma Giri two years ago, not knowing anything about it. I only knew it was something where you kept maun brat (silence). I was very fond of keeping maun bra—in fact I started practising maun brat about four years before I came to the course. You know we Punjabis have this system of "karva chauth", where you keep a fast for your husband's long life, and I decided no I wouldn't fast, I would keep a *maun*. And in that *maun* of one day, which was from six in the morning till nine at night, I started going very deep inside myself. I started feeling a peace I had never felt before. Normally I'm a very outgoing person. I'm a hairdresser and beautician by profession so I come in contact with a lot of women as well as men. Still I found this feeling of peace getting stronger and stronger.

I can just tell you one thing, friends, that coming here I have come to know that I am in tune with nature. It was the most exciting experience I could have gone through. I don't know why but I cry every time I say this. It's something from within that I was looking for, as we always pray to be in tune or at one with God. When I came here I found it was all within me, I didn't have to look outside at all for anything.

I went back home with complete happiness, with no fear in me, no hatred. I felt like a person cleansed from within, as if I were a bottle and someone had cleaned me with a brush so that I came out sparkling. I rang my husband in Mumbai after the course. He said "How are you?" And I said "I'm so happy, I can't tell you how happy I am!"

Since then I've been talking to my children and to my friends. They all are going to be coming here, in fact my daughter took a course earlier this year, and I want to spread this message, as everyone has been saying, especially to the children. That was the first thought that came to me—we've got to get the children to know themselves, because once you grow old, it is very difficult to open your mind. So I think we should work together to put the children first, to open their windows, so that they become better citizens.

Mrs Shahnaz Anand
Mumbai

❦❦❦

I learned that there are many in the audience who have not been able to find time to sit a Vipassana course, so I thought I would like to say a few words on how to find time for Vipassana.

I'm a businessman and economist from Nepal, so I'm used to seeing things from a cost-benefit point of view, trade-offs and so on. When you have a limited amount of money, you have to decide where to spend it. You have to sit down and figure out where it will provide most benefit, where it may even save money. Similarly, when you have a limited amount of time, you should also figure out where to spend that time to give maximum benefit and perhaps even to save time. I have received so many practical benefits from Vipassana.

I have found out the benefits of maintaining *sīla* (moral precepts), I rarely get angry or upset, so I don't waste time on these things. If wavering on a decision, *sīla* or Dharma shows me the way and I don't waste time. I am aware of my responsibilities and I feel I am more effective as a manager. I may raise my voice but I don't do it with anger or animosity. I have found that people take you much more seriously when you tell them what they have done wrong with a cool and calm mind, and what they should do to correct it—whether they are employees or your own children. So when you realise that Vipassana can give you so many benefits and also save you time, I'm sure it becomes easier to find the time to do a Vipassana course. We find time every day to clean our bodies, I'm sure that we can similarly find time to clean our minds.

These are some of the benefits you receive when you are living. Vipassana also helps you when you are dying. My father, Mani Harsh Jyoti, found out in July 1992 that he had lung cancer and he died in January 1993. During the last period of his life, I was able to observe him very closely. He was a serious Vipassana meditator. Every time he had a setback from the time of his diagnosis and during his treatment (which happened quite often), Vipassana helped him to restore his balance of mind and remain calm and peaceful. In his last few days I am sure it was with the help of Vipassana that he was able to give up his attachment to life. Observing him I felt that it was like putting water in a saucer and letting it evaporate; he passed away without a ripple. He passed away not only at peace with himself, but leaving so much peace around him, among his family and friends.

Many friends of mine, particularly my Rotarian friends, ask how I can find time to do regular ten-day courses and now even thirty-day or forty-five-day courses. I reply that if you had found out that you were going to have a heart attack or suffer a miserable death, and to avoid that you needed to spend ten days in a hospital, would you not make the time and admit yourself to the hospital? I look at Vipassana in the same way. If I don't spend time in meditation, I will lead a miserable life, maybe growing in misery day by day and perhaps suffering in death. So I just think of that and time for Vipassana is naturally found.

Mr Roop Jyoti
Businessman and Economist
Nepal

Taking a cue from our brother from Nepal and our sister from Punjab, I as a doctor I would like to point out that whenever we are acutely ill, physically ill, we never think twice about being admitted into hospital. But whenever it comes to the management of our own mind, we never even accept that we are ill, mentally ill, as we all undoubtedly are.

What does this mean? Unless we have developed in meditation, we find that whenever we sit down and close our eyes, we are never aware of where we are. Mentally we move out—into the past, into the future, and we are never really aware of this. We are never in the body where we should be. If this is a mental illness, every human being suffers from it. As a doctor I would like to tell you that during our five to eight years of medical training, we are never taught a single thing about the mind. Those who are called psychologists and psychiatrists are given some training in how to treat the diseases of someone else's mind. For instance, a psychologist may be able to advise a husband and wife with marital problems, but if the psychologist himself has a problem with his own wife, he won't know what to do. A good Vipassana meditator, whether a doctor or not, will know what to do because he knows how to watch his own mind.

The mind, with its tendency to move between past and future, never living in the present, can be compared to watching a television screen which is constantly showing replays of action, rather than the live action as it actually happens. To take another example, if you were asked where you stay, you might reply with this or that address which describes the place where you eat, sleep and to which the postman delivers your mail. In fact we constantly live only in our minds. Whether driving a car, at work or at home, I am in fact always in my mind and this is my common address. Vipassana gives us a way to watch this mind, to treat this sick mind. Those who have not taken a course, have the courage to take a ten-day retreat where you are the surgeon, you are the patient and you are the one who is going to walk out of the centre cured. To remain cured, you will have to continue the practice in daily life because of the many impurities our minds accumulate. Do not hesitate, the treatment is there and the hospital doors are open.

Dr H. N. Phadnis
Gynaecologist
Pune

We had a survey done this morning concerning the biggest identifiable problem facing humanity today. I am grateful that responses have come, not from all but many of you attending the seminar. The results of the survey show that the greatest single problem we face is that of ego and self-seeking. Next comes degeneration of national character; then jealousy, intolerance, fault-finding and ill will; then fear, apprehension about the future, insecurity. Then comes dishonesty and unruly behaviour; next lack of courage and conviction, lack of mental peace, corruption in life—how it prospers and people suffer.

The suggestions made to counteract these problems are: to inculçate selfless love; to take Vipassana to illiterate people in the villages, as they need it the most; to inculcate moral values in children in schools; and to inculcate it as well in the political elite who rule the country and set the pattern of behaviour for society.

Mr Ram Singh

Seminar Overview

N. Vaghul

It is difficult to sum up the very rich experiences of the last two days. For the sake of brevity I will just make a series of points giving a sense of what was achieved.

Objective of Seminar

The objective of the seminar was not to indulge in any intellectual debates on metaphysics, but to deal with the problems of society. It was not to find any mechanical solutions to the problems, but to test the hypothesis that Dharma can provide an alternative approach to solving these problems, and to draw up a specific action plan.

Definition of Dharma

To achieve these objectives, first we have to understand the meaning of the Dharma we are discussing. Someone mentioned that Dharma has different meanings in different contexts, and that the word is used thousands of times in the Pāli texts. For practical purposes, we are not so interested in all the different meanings, but we need to develop a common understanding of what we mean by Dharma, and that was provided in a very succinct and clear form by Goenkaji right at the outset of this seminar.

Let me refer to some points that he made.

* First, that Dharma is a path, a path of life.
* Secondly the essence of this path is twofold. One is to refrain from doing any act that causes hurt to other beings, and to perform acts which positively benefit other beings. The second is to free ourselves from all negativities by purifying the mind. Translated into specific action, what it means is that we eliminate craving or greed from our mind, we eschew negative feelings, we attain tranquillity and achieve perfect congruence between our thoughts, words and actions. That is whatever we do is to be in accordance with whatever we say, and whatever we say should be in accordance with what we think.
* It is not sufficient if we appreciate these elements merely at the intellectual level, they have to be appreciated at the experiential level.
* If the experience is to be valid and personal, there is no alternative but to work on yourself. This means you will have to delve deep within to find an answer. You cannot rely on hearsay; you cannot rely on any teachings, you will have find an answer from your own experience.

It is easy to say you will have to find an answer yourself, but you are dealing with a phenomenon which is subject to wild fluctuations, so a technique is needed to deal with this. Dealing with the mind is like trying to write on a blackboard which is hung right in the middle of a room, and which is swinging wildly. It is necessary to take the blackboard and fix it firmly to the wall, so it is stable and doesn't fluctuate, and to erase whatever is written on the board before you start writing on it.

Vipassana Technique

To work at the experiential level, what technique should be used? It is not claimed that this teaching of Vipassana is the only technique that could be used, but certainly Vipassana has shown the way. Apart from the fact that it dates back at least 2,500 years and has stood the test of time, it continues to be relevant in the modern world.

In the session before this one, people shared their experience of Vipassana. That session provided ample proof of the emotional experiences that people underwent during this whole mental exercise. Some had gone to one course, and others had done repeated courses. You heard about the immense benefit they had derived, even on the first attempt.

So Vipassana is a technique which can be used to achieve stability of mind, to eliminate mental impurities and to develop good moral qualities.

Non-Sectarian Nature of Dharma

Dharma is non-sectarian and universal. There was a good deal of debate on this point; it seems difficult to achieve consensus on the precise meaning of these terms.

I will give an example of a poet in Tamil Nadu in the fifth century by the name of Walluwar, who spoke of concepts which can be loosely equated to Dharma. Walluwar was claimed by the Buddhists who said his ideas were the same as those in the Buddhist texts. The Jains claimed they were the same as their teachings. A prominent Christian in the late nineteenth century said Walluwar must have taken up the ideas of the Christian mystics who had earlier settled down in that region. Hindus claim he was a Hindu and they put a sacred thread on his body in their images of him. I don't want to labour the point; you don't need any other evidence that the universal Dharma is the same: the universal Dharma.

Dharma and Science

We had an excellent presentation on whether Dharma is inconsistent with science. What emerged was, that these deal with two different domains: one with the physical domain of matter, the other with the spiritual dimension of non-matter. Notwithstanding that fact, Dharma has an independent claim as a science because it deals with the mind. Just because it does not deal with matter, you cannot call it unscientific. In the same way, you cannot say science is totally materialistic because science also has elements of humanism built into it. What emerged was, that we should not look at the two as opposite, but as complementary to each other. science cannot exist without Dharma, and Dharma cannot exist without science. Accordingly it is possible to achieve a unity between Dharma and Science, and examples were given where the current scientists of today are working towards this unity.

Social Problems

Now this brings us to the most important point of the seminar: how to deal with social problems. There was a very interesting presentation on social problems, which were divided into three major areas: political, social and economic.

At the political level we are confronted with the lust for office, the lust for power, and a tremendous amount of abuse of authority and power. Many instances were mentioned, showing how the politics of this country have degenerated.

There was also discussion of social problems: communal, caste and sectarian tensions, not only in India but around the world. Terrorism was mentioned, which is sweeping across many parts of the world; also noted was the violence presented in the media.

Then the economic problems were discussed, the problems of poverty and unemployment. One of the speakers mentioned that even the process of becoming rich has its problems. The process of liberalisation and globalisation that is occurring in this country is associated with the negative reactions of greed and craving that people have to deal with.

Why Current Solutions Don't Work

A very interesting paper was presented on the various mechanisms for dealing with these problems. There are the institutional structures of families, schools and charitable organisations. There are social welfare schemes that are being initiated by governments and government legislation which attempts to deal with social, communal and caste tensions. Science and technology is coming forward to find solutions, to enrich and uplift our lives. Many alternatives have been found to make life more comfortable than it used to be. Finally there are world multi-lateral organisations, like the United Nations, which are trying to deal with terrorism, global poverty, slums and so on.

The ineffectiveness of dealing with these problems in this way has been highlighted, because in all of these cases, there have been only limited improvements. An analysis showed that there are two reasons that we have not been able to deal effectively with these problems.

Firstly, we have only dealt with the symptoms, the outward manifestations of these problems; we are not dealing with the underlying causes. What happens is, the problems may seem to disappear, but as the underlying malady persists, the symptoms keep appearing again and again. The underlying malady, as has been pointed out so often during our discussions, is the greed, the jealousy, and the negative feelings that permeate the world. These are the real cause of all the social, political and economic problems that we confront.

Secondly, the feeling was that the people whose task it is to implement solutions through social structures and legislation don't have the necessary love and compassion. For example, in India there are so many anti-poverty programs initiated by the government, and their implementation has been entrusted to various government organisations. These organisations deal with the problems in a very mechanical way, there is a lot of waste and leakage in the system, and the gains do not go to the intended beneficiaries.

I think the problems can be tackled at two levels. Ultimately the solution has to be found at the individual level. Each of us has to work on ourselves in a sustained campaign to remove the craving, greed and negativity. Secondly, at the institutional level we need to encourage a Dharmic way of working.

Action Plan

This leads us to the last point of our discussions—a specific action plan. As was outlined in the session on social problems, we have to deal with these problems at the individual level. Now are we really going to take on the responsibility of converting the whole world of five billion people into a Dharmic way of life? As far as we know, it has never happened in the past, that all the people in the world were converted in this way. I think we should be humble enough to recognize our limitations. What I think we need to do is transform the critical mass of the people, who really make a difference. If we succeed in transforming this critical mass of people into the Dharmic way of life, by exposing them to the concepts of Vipassana, then we will have taken the first step towards the transformation of the community.

Four intervention points were mentioned.

a) Schools and colleges. Right from the level of primary education, we need to inculcate this way of life. A variety of techniques can be used. One example was given of a teacher in Germany who was able to achieve a great improvement in the concentration and attitude of his students, by asking them to do five minutes of Anapana meditation before starting a lesson. Mr Bordia mentioned about the possibility of introducing teachers to Vipassana. In this way we can more readily transform the children and initiate an enduring process of reform in our educational system.

b) Work Organisations. Moving into the corporate sector, we need to transform the "king-pins" of the economic system, the corporate executives and managers, by exposing them to Vipassana.

c) Bureaucracy. We need to identify the people who really matter to the economy, administration and to the community.

d) Political system. Again a transformation is needed in these key people.

While continuing to operate at the individual level, with this critical mass of people, we must go beyond that to the institutional level: corporate, bureaucratic and political institutions. We need to do some more research into how the way of working of important institutions can undergo a Dharmic transformation. We need to find ways in which a sense of values can be imparted, so that the moral principles which form the foundation of Dharma can be practised.

On that note we ended, with a substantial platform upon which to build our future actions. We believe that this seminar has been immensely successful and has provided us with the necessary impetus to carry this message forward.

Excerpts from Closing Talk

S. N. Goenka

Venerable Monks and Dharma friends:

For the last two days you have been discussing the use of Dharma in improving society—a very important subject. Unless something is done to solve social problems, misery will keep on increasing. But to improve society we cannot forget the individual; Man matters most. And to improve the individual, we cannot forget the mind; mind matters most.

To improve the mind Dharma is the only tool, and it must be applied Dharma.

You have rightly pointed out at the conclusion of your seminar that actual, practical steps have to be taken. Mere sermons will not do. Our country does not lack in sermons. We have been listening to them for ages; they go in one ear and out the other. We say, "Wonderful. This is very good." But how do we apply Dharma in life?

It is necessary to deal with the individual and the mind of the individual. This is a big task. There are billions of people around the world, and hundreds of millions in this country; will they be able to practise Vipassana? I am very optimistic.

Emperor Aśoka

The technique of Vipassana disappeared from India about five hundred years after the time of the Buddha. But the rock edicts of Emperor Aśoka show that during his reign the Dhamma flourished. That is why Aśoka is acknowledged as one of the greatest rulers in the history of the world.

In these inscriptions, Aśoka proclaimed that, like all rulers before him, he wanted his subjects to live in harmony, to live a life of Dhamma, and to have respect for their elders and love for those younger. Similarly, he wanted the different religious sects to be on friendly terms with one another. Unlike his predecessors, Aśoka attained these goals.

He maintained that he had succeeded because he spread the wonderful teaching of the Dhamma—the practice of meditation—throughout the country. He had *dhammāmatyas* [Dhamma teachers] travel to different parts of the kingdom to explain the teaching. They did not convert people from one religion to another. In fact it appears that, for five hundred years after Buddha, nobody used the word *bauddha-dharma* [Buddhist Dhamma]. They said only "Dhamma."

Every edict of Aśoka speaks only of the Dhamma. The people were taught not only the theory of the Dhamma but also the practice of meditation, and so they became peaceful and happy. Aśoka claimed that his success was demonstrated by an improvement in the moral conduct of his people. If this were not true, surely the rock edicts would have been smashed long ago. But they have survived for 2,200 years.

The inscriptions testify to the mass application of this technique, with the result of profound changes in society at that time.

We have to find out how Aśoka succeeded in taking Vipassana to every part of the country. The teachers he appointed taught all levels of society, from the royal family to the poorest of the poor. We have to find out how to do this now.

People at the Helm of Affairs

If it is possible, we should start with people of the elite. All good or bad things trickle down from the top and then spread through the whole society.

But how will these people be attracted? There are promising results from the work done over the last twenty-five years. Of course there are those who have doubts, but people have started thinking that there must be something in Vipassana. I am sure a time will come, sooner rather than later, when the people at the helm of affairs will come to find out what it is.

There is misery everywhere, even for those of the elite. I would say they are more miserable than anyone else. Leaders of the business community (I have been one myself and I know how miserable these people are), political leaders (I have been very close to them in Burma, and here also I hear and see)—they are very miserable.

Similarly in every sector of society, those who are at the top are really miserable. Like anyone else, they need peace and harmony within. If they come to know that there is a way they can experience peace and harmony within themselves and help the surrounding atmosphere to be peaceful and harmonious, certainly they will become attracted; but it may take some time.

The Coming Generation

You have rightly concluded that we should work with the coming generation. Vipassana must go to the young. I have seen that those studying at schools and colleges are accepting it and getting good results. Their memory becomes very strong, their comprehension is much improved and (another important thing) their nervousness goes away.

A student might have learned a subject well, but at examination time he or she becomes anxious, forgets everything and gets low marks or even fails. With this technique we advise simply to practise two minutes of Anapana, to observe respiration, before opening the question paper. The mind calms down and then the students answer their papers. Very good results are emerging.

I have seen that when you talk to boys and girls of the new generation about Dharma, they ask, "What Dharma?" They see that their parents go to temples, mosques or churches without any change in themselves. When they see that their parents' entire way of living is immoral, they lose interest in Dharma. But they are attracted to it when they come to know that Dharma is scientific, rational and pragmatic, giving results here and now,

I have noticed that members of the younger generation accept Dharma, true Dharma, more easily than their elders. Character building should start at a young age. I am very happy that this seminar has come to the conclusion that this wonderful technique should go to students in schools and colleges.

The Scriptures

Yesterday I was told that there was an interesting discussion about the meaning of the word Dharma, what the scriptures say, and what the meaning is according to the scriptures.

I smiled on hearing this. I also know from my own experience that most people do not understand at all. Even Buddha's words, wherever they are taught in schools or in colleges, are learned merely to obtain a certificate.

We took up the responsibility of publishing the words of the Buddha because they contain so many fine points about Dharma and the practice of Vipassana. But these can be understood only by real practice. *Dhammaniyāmatā* is the law of nature, but if one is trying to understand only at the intellectual level, it won't have the same meaning.

You must purify your mind, the totality of the mind. If you are simply answering questions for school or college, to get high marks, there will be no understanding of Vipassana. When you practise, every word will carry a different meaning altogether. Not only the words of the Buddha, but every scripture will carry a different meaning.

In my experience during the last twenty-six years in India, a large number of Christian priests have come to courses. The first mother superior who joined a course, Mother Mary, said, "You are teaching Christianity in the name of the Buddha!" Yes, I am teaching Christianity in the name of the Buddha.

A very learned mullah who participated in a course in a mosque said afterwards, "There are two *Āyāts* of the Koran which we could not understand, but now their meaning has become so clear through this practice." The *Āyāts* say, "One who observes the respiration and observes properly will observe Allah. One who observes the body and observes properly will observe Allah." The mullah said that he had been reading these texts, but could not see what Allah had to do with respiration, and every day when taking a bath he could see the whole of his body, but he could not see Allah. He and fellow scholars knew there must be some special meaning, but they could not find it. He told me, "Oh, now we understand."

People from the Sikh community have come and they say, "We did not understand the real intent of the words spoken by the saints and Gurus. With Vipassana we understand their real meaning and purport."

I come from an orthodox Hindu family. I used to recite the *Gītā*, and after passing through this process of Vipassana, every word carried a different meaning altogether. I had my own understanding before, but after I started practising Vipassana, I found a totally different meaning.

The same may be said of the words of the Buddha, which explain Vipassana, the law of nature and the scientific Dhamma so clearly. The people of India had lost the words of the Buddha, and so (although teaching Vipassana meditation remains my main responsibility), I took the decision to publish them. Fortunately we have scholars to ensure that the publication is exactly as accepted by the Sixth Council. The publication should be perfect.

I am happy that these scholars are taking an interest in Vipassana. I am confident that they will soon start saying, "Oh, a Vipassana meditator will understand the meaning of this; it can't be a dictionary meaning, it must be an experiential meaning."

The publication of the theoretical aspect of Dharma is being undertaken to allow the practical aspect of Dharma to be properly checked, and to inspire people to practise. Actual experience alone will help us. If this becomes merely an academic organisation, publishing Pāli texts, and we keep arguing about this word or that without tasting Dharma, it will be valueless. Real benefits will come only from practice, nothing else.

Dharma is Non-Sectarian

Now people are recognising this, and they are giving importance to the real practice of Dharma without making it sectarian.

If my teacher had said to me before my first course, "I am going to make you a Buddhist," I would have been the last person to go to him. My teacher taught me real Dhamma, the law universal, and I found what I was looking for. When I passed through the ten days I discovered to my great joy, "Oh, this is applied *Gītā*, not merely theories. This is how one can become *vītarāga* [free from passion], *vītadveṣa* [free from anger], *vīta bhaya* [free from fear]. One can become *stitha prajña* [firm in judgement and wisdom]."

The technique can benefit everyone. Hindus, Muslims, Christians, Jains can all practise and continue to regard themselves as followers of their own religions; it makes no difference. Unless one becomes a good human being, how can one be a good Hindu, or a good Muslim, or a good Buddhist, or a good Jain? Dharma teaches us how to become good human beings, not by sermons but by actual practice.

I am fortunate I came into contact with this wonderful path. From it I have received far greater benefits than I could ever have expected. Naturally I wish to share the path with others, but not with the intention of converting people to another religion. That would not help at all and would create more barriers. Let people understand that Dharma is universal, that it is not tied to any particular sect.

Of course, when we discuss Vipassana we use the name of Buddha. Sometimes because of conditioning, people will ask, "This sounds Buddhist, why do you talk of the Buddha?" I smile.

Why do I talk of the Buddha? When teaching science and talking about the law of gravity, we say that Newton discovered it, and we may call it Newton's Law of Gravity. Of course the law of gravity was there, whether we knew it or not, with Newton or without Newton, and in future the law will remain the same. Similarly with Dharma: it was there and someone discovered it. Should we not be grateful to him?

The Buddha said, *Tumhehi kiccaṃ ātappaṃ akkhātāro tathāgatā*. You have to walk every step of the path yourself; you have to work for your own salvation. An enlightened one will only show the path because he has walked over it. He cannot liberate you; no-one can do that.

I am glad that people have started understanding; although their number is small, that doesn't matter. There is great darkness all around. Even with one lamp lit, we are happy to have a small circle of light. Soon this one lamp will become two and then three lamps, and in this way the Dhamma will spread. And with the use of modern scientific facilities, whatever you are now proposing can happen. If it could happen in the days of Aśoka, when all these facilities did not exist, why should it not happen now? It will happen, I am sure.

May all of you who have come to discuss Dharma in this seminar get inspiration to taste Dharma, and live a happy, harmonious life, good for you and for all others.

Dharma and Sectarianism

A Public Talk by S. N. Goenka

Dharma and Sectarianism

A Public Talk by S. N. Goenka

Dharma and Sectarianism

A Public Talk by S. N. Goenka

Friends, seekers of peace and harmony:

Everyone seeks peace. Everyone seeks harmony. Life is full of misery, misery of one kind or another, due to this reason or that reason. There is misery everywhere. How can we come out of misery? How can we live peaceful, harmonious lives, good for ourselves and good for others?

The sages, saints and seers of India_the wise, enlightened ones_asked: "Why is there misery?" and "Is there a way out of misery?" There are innumerable apparent reasons why there is misery. But we cannot come out of misery by eradicating these apparent reasons. The real cause of misery lies deep within ourselves. And unless this deep-rooted cause of misery is eradicated, we can never experience real peace, real harmony or real happiness.

How can we eradicate the deep-rooted cause of misery within ourselves? Everyone who was wise and enlightened realized that the only way to eradicate misery was by following the path of Dharma. If one lives the life of Dharma, one is definitely coming out of misery. Dharma and misery cannot co-exist. But the difficulty came when, after a few centuries, people forgot what Dharma was. When one does not understand the real meaning of Dharma, how can one apply Dharma in life?

Two thousand years ago in India, there were two distinct traditions. One tradition gave importance to the purity of Dharma. The other gave importance to sectarian rites, rituals, religious ceremonies, external appearances, and so on. In those days the tradition of pure Dharma was quite strong, but slowly it became weaker and weaker, and eventually vanished from India. What was left had no trace of pure Dharma. It is very unfortunate that we have lost Dharma. When one speaks of Dharma in today's India, the question that arises in the audience's mind is: "Which Dharma? Hindu-dharma, Buddhist-dharma, Jain-dharma, Christian-dharma, Muslim-dharma, Sikh-dharma, Parsi-dharma, or Jewish-dharma? Which Dharma?"

It is a great pity that we have totally forgotten pure Dharma. How can Dharma be Hindu, Muslim, Christian, Jain, Parsi, or Sikh? This is impossible. If Dharma is pure Dharma, it is universal. It cannot be sectarian. Sectarian rites and rituals differ from one sect to another. The so-called "Hindu-dharma" has its own rites, rituals and religious ceromonies; its own beliefs, dogmas, and philosophies; and its own external appearances, and disciplines, such as fasting. It is the same with the Muslim-dharma, Christian-dharma, Sikh-dharma, and so on. But Dharma has nothing to do with all these. Sectarianism is divisive. Dharma is universal: it unites.

The meaning of Dharma in the ancient language of India has been lost. Unfortunately, our country has lost the bulk of its ancient literature and scriptures. This literature was preserved and is still being maintained in the neighbouring countries. When we study these writings it becomes so clear what the people of this country meant by Dharma in ancient times. The definition was *"Dhāret¨ ti dharma"*—what one holds, what one contains, is Dharma. This means what one's mind is holding, what one's mind is containing, at this moment. These contents may be wholesome thoughts, or unwholesome thoughts. In the language of those days, wholesome thoughts were called kuoala-dharma, and unwholesome thoughts were called akuoala-dharma. We find that these two words were used for a long time in our ancient literature. Kuoala-dharma and akuoala-dharma are both Dharma. What one's mind contains at this moment is Dharma_"Dhāret¨ ti dharma."

Two other words that occur in the ancient literature are ārya-dharma and anārya-dharma. As the centuries passed, the real meaning of these words has been lost. Today the word ārya is used for a particular race of human beings. In the India of those days, this meaning was nowhere to be found. ṭrya had nothing to do with a race of human beings. Rather, it meant one who has a pure mind_one who is a noble person, a saintly person; one who has eradicated all the impurities of the mind. Such a one was called an ārya. One who lives the life of negativity, impurity, and generates anger, hatred, ill will, or animosity, was called anārya. So anybody whose mind contained purity was called ārya, and anybody whose mind contained impurity was called anārya.

Words like Hindu-dharma, Buddhist-dharma or Jain-dharma, were never used in our ancient literature. Other sects came much later, but even when these three were there, nobody used these words. The words kuoala-dharma and akuoala-dharma were used. Slowly, after a few centuries, another division came: kuoala-dharma (wholesome Dharma) was called dharma, and akuoala-dharma (unwholesome Dharma) was called adharma.

In the ancient scriptures, there was another definition of the word dharma: the nature or characteristic of what the mind contains, whether wholesome or unwholesome. What is the characteristic of the contents of one's mind? This was called dharma. Its nature, its characteristic was called dharma. In Indian languages today, we still hear an echo of this meaning when someone says: "The dharma of fire is to burn." The nature of fire is to burn itself and to burn others. Similarly, we can say that the dharma of ice is to create coolness. This is the nature of ice.

What do these universal characteristics have to do with Hinduism? What have they to do with Buddhism, or Christianity, Islam, Jainism or Sikhism? Fire burns; ice cools. This is a universal law of nature. If fire does not burn itself and others, it cannot be fire. If it is fire, then its characteristic must be to burn itself and to burn others. The dharma of the sun is to give light and heat. If it does not give light and heat, it cannot be the sun. The dharma of the moon is to give a soft, cool light. This is the dharma, the nature of the moon. If it does not do that, it is not the moon.

This was how the word dharma was used in those days. If the contents of my mind are unwholesome_for example, if I am generating anger, hatred, ill will, or animosity at this moment_then the nature of these negativities is to burn. They will burn me. The vessel containing the fire is the fire's first victim; then this fire and its heat start spreading to the environment around it.

It is the same when there is negativity in the mind. One who contains this negativity, who generates this negativity, is the first victim. He or she becomes very miserable. How can you expect peace, harmony and happiness, if you are generating anger? This is totally against the law of nature. That means it is totally against Dharma, which is the universal law of nature. If, knowingly or unknowingly, I place my hand in fire, my hand is bound to burn. The fire does not discriminate. It does not notice whether the hand belongs to a person who calls himself or herself a Hindu, Muslim, Christian, Jain, Sikh or Parsi, or an Indian, American, Russian or Chinese. There is no difference, no discrimination, no partiality; Dharma is Dharma.

In the same way, when my mind is generating purity, the negativities are eradicated. According to the law of nature, when the mind is pure, it is full of love, compassion, sympathetic joy and equanimity. This is the nature of a pure mind. This pure mind may belong to a Hindu or a Christian, or it may belong to an Indian or a Pakistani: it makes no difference at all. If the mind is pure, it must have these qualities. And when the mind is full of love, compassion, goodwill and equanimity, then again, the universal law is such that these contents of the mind have their own nature, their own Dharma. They give so much peace, so much harmony, so much happiness. One may keep calling oneself by any name. He may keep performing this rite or that ritual, this religious ceromony or that religious ceremony. He may have this external appearance or that external appearance. He may believe in this philosophy or that philosophy. It makes no difference at all. Dharma is Dharma.

The moment you defile your mind, the moment you generate any negativity, nature starts punishing you then and there. The punishment doesn't wait until after death. Whatever happens after death will happen then. But what happens now? Anybody who generates anger now will experience nothing but unhappiness and misery. This person may have any name, may be from any caste, from any community, from any sect or from any country: it makes no difference at all. Because one has generated negativity, one is bound to suffer here and now.

Similarly, when you generate purity of mind, when your mind is full of good qualities such as love, compassion and goodwill, nature starts rewarding you here and now. You won't have to wait until the end of your life_you start getting the rewards of a pure mind now. When your mind is full of love, full of compassion, you start experiencing so much peace, harmony and happiness. This is Dharma. It has nothing to do with sectarianism.

Someone who calls himself a very staunch Hindu, a staunch Muslim, a staunch Christian or a staunch Sikh, may be a very good Dharmic person, or may not have any trace of Dharma. Sectarian rites and rituals, sectarian beliefs or philosophies, sectarian religious ceremonies and outward appearances have nothing to do with Dharma. Dharma is totally different. Dharma means what your mind contains now. If what it contains is wholesome, it rewards you. If it is unwholesome, it punishes you.

If this understanding of Dharma becomes more and more prevalent in Indian society, as it was twenty-five centuries ago, then the country will be more peaceful because its people will be more peaceful. Everyone will give importance to whether or not he or she is a Dharmic person. That means, is one keeping one's mind pure, free from impurities, free from negativities? If you keep generating anger, hatred, ill will, animosity and other negativities, you are not a Dharmic person. You may perform some rite or ritual. You may go to a temple and bow before a particular idol, or to a mosque to recite a namaz. You may go to a church to say prayers, or to a gurudwārā to chant kirtans. Or you may go to a pagoda and pay respect to the statue of Buddha. These do not help at all.

When you generate negativity in your mind, you may blame various outside reasons for your misery. You may find fault with others. You may be under the wrong impression that you are miserable because so-and-so abused or insulted you, or because something which you wanted has not happened, or because something that you did not want has happened. You remain deluded for your whole life that you are miserable because of these apparent external reasons. Because Dharma was lost to the country, we have forgotten to go deep inside to find the real cause of misery.

Suppose someone abuses me, and I become miserable. Between these two events, something very important happens inside me. But that link remains unknown to me. When somebody abuses me, I start generating anger and hatred; I start reacting with negativity. Only then do I become miserable, not before. The reason I am miserable is not because somebody has abused me, nor because something unwanted has happened. Rather, it is because I am reacting to these outside things. This is the real cause of my misery. You cannot understand this by listening to discourses such as this, by reading scriptures, by intellectualizing or accepting it at the emotional or devotional level. The real understanding of Dharma can only come when you start experiencing it within yourself.

To illustrate this point: suppose by mistake I have placed my hand in fire. The law of nature is such that the fire starts burning my hand. I take my hand away because I don't like being burned. The next time, I again make a mistake and put my hand in the fire. Again, my hand gets burned, and again I take my hand back. I may do this once, twice, or three times, and then I start to understand: "This is fire, and the nature of fire is to burn. So I had better not touch the fire." This becomes a lesson, and I begin to understand at the experiential level that I must keep my hand away from fire.

In a similar way, one can learn how to practise Dharma using a technique which was very common in ancient India. To learn Dharma means to observe the reality within oneself. The word that was used for this was "vipassanā," which means "to observe reality in a special way." This means to observe reality in the right way, the correct way, to observe it as it is_not just as it appears to be, not just as it seems to be, not coloured by any belief or philosophy, not coloured by any imagination_but to observe it by working in a scientific way.

For example, when anger has arisen, you observe the reality that anger has arisen. Cutting yourself off from the external object of anger, you simply observe anger as anger, hatred as hatred; or passion as passion, ego as ego. You observe any impurity that has arisen on the mind. You simply observe it, observe it objectively, without identifying yourself with that particular negativity.

It is very difficult to observe objectively. When anger arises, it is like a volcanic eruption, and we get overpowered by it. When we are overpowered by anger, we cannot observe anger. Instead, we perform all the vocal and physical actions which we did not want to perform. And then we keep repenting: "I should not have done this. I should not have reacted in this way." But the next time a similar situation occurs, we will react in the same way, because we have not experienced the truth within ourselves.

If you learn this technique of observing the reality within yourself, then you will notice that, as anger arises in the mind, two things start happening simultaneously at the physical level. At a gross level_at the level of your breath_you will notice that, as soon as anger, hatred, ill will, passion, ego, or any impurity arises in the mind, your breath loses its normality. It cannot remain normal. It will become abnormal_slightly hard, slightly fast. And once that particular negativity has gone away, you will notice that your breath becomes normal. It is no longer fast, no longer hard. This happens in the physical structure at a gross level.

Something also happens at a subtler level, because mind and matter are so interrelated. One keeps influencing the other, and getting influenced by the other. This interaction is continuously happening within ourselves, day and night. At a subtler level a biochemical reaction starts within the physical structure. An electromagnetic reaction starts and, if you are a good Vipassana meditator, you will notice: "Look, anger has arisen." And then what happens? There is heat throughout the body; there is palpitation; there is tension throughout the body.

One need not do anything except observe. Do nothing; just observe. Don't try to push out your anger. Don't try to push out the signs of the anger. Just observe, just observe. Continue to observe, and you will notice that the anger becomes weaker and weaker, and passes away. If you suppress it, then it goes deep into the subconscious level of your mind. When it is suppressed, it does not pass away.

Whenever misery comes, we think that the cause of this misery is something outside, and we make a great effort to rectify external things: "So-and-so is misbehaving. I am unhappy because of this person's misbehaviour. When this person stops misbehaving, I will be a very happy person." We want to change this person. Is this possible? Can we change others? Well, even if we succeed in changing one person, what guarantee is there that somebody else will not appear, who will again go totally against our desires? It is impossible to change the entire world. The saints and sages, enlightened people, discovered the way out: change yourself. Let anything happen outside, but do not react. Observe the truth as it is. But when we don't know the technique of observing ourselves_the technique of self-realization, the technique of truth-realization_then we can't work out our own salvation.

For example, you may try to divert your attention. You are very miserable and you can't change the other person or the outside situation, so you try to divert your mind. You go to a cinema or a theatre, or worse, to a bar or gambling casino, to divert your attention. For awhile you may feel that your misery is gone. This is an illusion: you have not come out of your misery; it is still there. You have merely diverted your attention, and the misery has gone deep inside. Time and time again it will erupt and overpower you. You have not come out of your misery.

There is another way of diverting the mind, this time in the name of religion. You go to a temple, a mosque, a gurudwārā, or a pagoda, to chant or pray. Your mind will be diverted, and you may feel quite happy. But again, this is an escape. You are not facing your problem. This was not the Dharma of ancient India.

We have to face the problem. When misery arises in the mind, face it. By observing it objectively, you go to the deepest cause of misery. If you can learn to observe the deepest cause of misery, you will find that layers of this deep-rooted cause start getting eradicated. As layer after layer gets peeled off, you start to be relieved of your misery. You have neither suppressed your negativity, nor expressed it at the vocal or physical level and harmed others. You have observed it. Doing nothing, you have just observed.

This is a wonderful technique of India. Unfortunately, our country lost it because we lost the real meaning of the word dharma. Now these crutches, these scaffoldings of Hindu-dharma, Buddhist-dharma, Jain-dharma and Muslim-dharma have become predominant for us. When we say Hindu-dharma, then Hindu is predominant for us. Poor Dharma recedes behind the curtain into the darkness. Dharma has no value, because Hindu is more important. When we say Muslim-dharma, Muslim is important. When we say Buddhist-dharma, Buddhist is important; Jain-dharma, Jain is important. It's as if Dharma is not an entity of its own. But what a great entity Dharma is! It is the law of nature, the eternal truth; and we are missing it when we give prominence to these false scaffoldings, crutches. We are forgetting the real essence of Dharma.

When someone starts giving importance to Hindu-dharma, he never gives importance to Dharma. Hindu-dharma and all the rites, rituals, ceremonies and appearances become more important for this person. He performs them and feels that he is a very Dharmic person. Similarly, if one gives importance to Muslim-dharma, Sikh-dharma, or Buddhist-dharma, one feels that he is a very Dharmic person. This person may not have even a trace of Dharma, because all the time his mind is full of impurity, full of negativity. What a great delusion it is when one feels that he is a Dharmic person because he has performed his rite or ritual; because he has gone to this temple or to that mosque; because he has gone to this church or to that gurudwārā; because he has recited this or recited that. What has happened to us? Where is this sectarianism leading us? Far away from Dharma!

The yardstick of Dharma should be: "Is my mind getting purified or not?" There is nothing wrong with performing a particular rite, ritual, or religious ceremony. There is nothing wrong with going to a mosque or a temple. But one should keep examining oneself to see: "Is my mind getting purified by performing all these rites, rituals and ceremonies? Am I getting liberated from anger, hatred, ill will, animosity, passion, ego?" If so, then yes, they are very good.

If no improvement is coming, then one sees that he is just deluding himself, fooling himself: "Even if my mind appears to be purified for a short time, I am deluding myself, because I have not come out of my misery, my impurities. My impurities lie at the deepest unconscious level of my mind. That is the storehouse of my impurities." We carry this storehouse from life to life, from life to life. And we either give more input, more impurities, or we remove them.

Mostly we keep giving more and more input, and therefore we become more and more miserable. How can we purify the deepest level of the mind? We can purify the surface of the mind to some extent by intellectualizing, or by devotional or emotional beliefs. But to take out the impurities from the deepest level of the mind, we have to work_and work in the way that nature wants us to work. The law of nature says that whenever we generate any impurity, the source of the impurity lies at the deepest level of our mind. And the deepest level of our mind is constantly in contact with body sensations.

Day and night, whether you are asleep or awake, the deepest level of your mind (the so-called "unconscious") is never unconscious: it is always feeling sensations on the body. Whenever there is a pleasant sensation, it will react with craving_rāga, rāga. Whenever there is an unpleasant sensation, it will react with aversion_dveOha, dveOha. Craving, aversion, craving, aversion: this has become the behaviour pattern of the mind deep inside. Twenty-four hours a day, day and night, every moment there are sensations in the body deep inside, and at the deepest level the mind keeps reacting. It has become a slave of its own behaviour pattern. Unless we break that slavery, how can we come out of our misery? We will be just deluding ourselves by trying to purify the surface of the mind, while we forget the deep root. As long as the roots are impure, the mind can never become pure.

Vipassana is a technique of India. Laudable references to Vipassana are given in the `g Veda. The most ancient literature of this country is full of words of praise for Vipassana:

Yo viovābhih vipaoyati bhuvanah

sañca paoyati sa na pāroadati dvioah.

One who practises Vipassana in a perfect way_sañca paoyati, sa na pāroadati dvioah_comes out of all aversion and anger; the mind becomes pure.

But one has to practise it oneself. If you just keep reciting this verse of the `g Veda, how is this going to help? Suppose you keep reciting: "The cake is very sweet; the cake is very sweet." How can you taste the sweetness of the cake unless you put it in your mouth? The practice of Dharma is more important than merely accepting Dharma at the intellectual, emotional or devotional level. And this practice is Vipassana.

In ancient days, Vipassana was everywhere in India. A traveller came from Burma then. Travelling the whole country, he found that in every household people were practising Vipassana. He visited different households, rich and poor, and found that not only the husband, wife and children, but even the servants were practising Vipassana every morning and evening. And everywhere there was talk of Vipassana, because people were getting benefit from it. Over time, unfortunately, in this country we became involved in rites, rituals and religious ceremonies and forgot this scientific understanding of Dharma.

Dharma is nothing but a pure science, a super-science of mind and matter: the interaction of mind and matter, the cross-currents and the under-currents happening deep inside every moment. Things are happening inside every moment, but we remain extroverted, giving importance to things outside. Say somebody has abused me, and I don't have this practice of observing what is happening within myself: I become angry and start shouting. What am I doing?

When someone is abusing me, it is that person's problem, not mine. If they are abusing, it means that they are generating negativity in the mind. This person is a sick person, an unhappy person, a miserable person when he is generating anger and shouting. Why should I generate anger? Why should I shout and make myself miserable? This understanding cannot come unless you have experienced it. It is like the experience when you touch fire and learn not to touch it again. It happens once, twice, several times, and then you learn not to touch fire again. Similarly, you can develop the ability to observe what is happening inside. Anger has arisen and you will immediately notice that there is fire, and it has started burning you: "Look, I am burning! I don't like burning. Next time I will be more careful." Or, "Oh no, here is anger. If I generate anger, I'll burn." By mistake you have again generated anger; again you observe it. Again you generate anger, and again you observe it. After a few experiences, you start coming out of it.

But when you are not observing the reality within yourself, then you give all importance to the apparent external cause of your misery, trying to rectify that. For example, a mother-in-law says: "Our household is a real hell now." If you ask her the reason, she says: "It is all because of this daughter-in-law. What a daughter-in-law has come into our house! She is so modernized. She goes totally against all our traditions and beliefs! She has spoiled the entire harmony of the household." If you talk to the daughter-in-law, she will say: "The old lady should change a little. She doesn't understand that there is a generation gap. The times are changing. Why doesn't she understand? She is making herself and everybody else miserable." The daughter-in-law wants the mother-in-law to change. The mother-in-law wants the daughter-in-law to change. The father wants the son to change. The son wants the father to change. This brother wants the other brother to change. The other brother wants this brother to change.

"I won't change. I am perfectly all right. Nothing in me needs changing!" We never see within ourselves that we are not perfectly all right, that we are the cause of our own misery. The basic problem lies within ourselves, not outside. We start realizing this at the experiential level by practising Vipassana. It is very difficult to observe abstract anger. Even for a Vipassana meditator, it takes a long time before one reaches the stage where one can observe abstract anger, or abstract passion, abstract fear, abstract ego. It is very difficult.

When anger arises, along with it, a sensation starts in the body. Along with anger, the breath also becomes abnormal. You can observe this. Even in ten days you can learn this technique. By coming to a Vipassana course and working properly, you can understand how to observe the breath. Perhaps anger has come, and you can't observe abstract anger, but you can observe your breath: "Look, the breath is coming in and going out." This is not a breathing exercise. You just observe the breath as it is_if it is shallow, it is shallow; if it is deep, it is deep; if it passes through the left nostril, then the left nostril; through the right nostril, then the right nostril. You simply observe it. Or perhaps there is heat throughout the body, or palpitation, or tension. You just observe them. It is easy. These things become easy to observe if you practise even for one or two ten-day courses.

To observe anger as anger, or hatred as hatred, or passion as passion, is very difficult. It takes time. That is why the wise people, the enlightened people, the saints and seers of India advised: "Observe yourself." Observing oneself is a path of self-realization, truth-realization_one can even say "God-realization," because after all, truth is God. What else is God? The law is God, nature is God. And when one is observing that law; one is observing Dharma. Whatever is happening within you, you are just a silent observer, not reacting. As you observe objectively, you have started taking the first step to understand Dharma; the first step towards practising Dharma in life.

By practising Dharma, you won't run away from external activities like going to this or that temple, or performing this or that rite or ritual. But at the same time as you are doing these things, you will start observing the reality pertaining to your mind at that moment: "What is happening in my mind at this moment? Whatever is happening in my mind from moment to moment_this is more important for me than anything that is happening outside." You will start to notice how are you reacting to things outside. Whenever you react, this reaction becomes a source of misery for you. If you learn not to react but simply to observe, you will come out of the suffering. Of course it takes time. One does not become perfect immediately, but a beginning is made.

Let a beginning be made to understand Dharma. Dharma is free from all sectarian beliefs, dogmas, rites and rituals. Even sectarian names are not necessary. You may or may not call yourself a Hindu or a Muslim, but you should be a Dharmic person, a person living the life of Dharma. This means that your mind should remain pure. If your mind remains pure, then all your other actions, vocal or physical, will naturally become pure.

Mind is the base. When the mind is impure, full of negativities, then our vocal actions are bound to be impure, and our physical actions are bound to be impure. We have started harming ourselves. We have started harming others. As I said, when you generate anger, or hatred, or ill will, you are the first victim of your negativity. You become very miserable, and the misery that you generate because of your negativity starts to permeate the atmosphere around you. The entire environment around you becomes so tense. Anyone who comes in contact with you at that time becomes tense, miserable. You are distributing your misery to others. This is what you have, and you keep distributing it to others. You are making yourself miserable, and you are making others miserable.

On the other hand, if you learn the art of Dharma_this means the art of living_and you stop generating negativity, you start experiencing peace and harmony within yourself. When you keep your mind pure, full of love and compassion, the peace and harmony that is generated within permeates the atmosphere around you. Anyone who comes in contact with you at that time starts experiencing peace and harmony. You are distributing something good that you have. You have peace, you have harmony, you have real happiness, and you are distributing this to others. This is Dharma, the art of living.

In ancient India, Dharma was nothing but an art of living, the art of how to live peacefully and harmoniously within, and how to generate nothing but peace and harmony for others. And to achieve that, proper training was given. There were Vipassana meditation centres in practically every village. Vipassana centres were everywhere, as were yoga schools, yoga colleges and yoga hospitals. They were a part of life. Students used to learn this art in their schooling. Practising it, they lived good lives, healthy lives, harmonious lives.

May that era come again. May people understand what Dharma is. May you be released from the demons, the devils, of sectarianism and communalism which make you forget all about Dharma. May you come out of this suffering. May you live a real life of Dharma, so peaceful, harmonious and happy for you and so peaceful, harmonious and happy for others.

May all of you who have come to this Dharma talk find time to spare ten days of your life to learn this technique. You will get the benefits here and now. It is not necessary for you to convert yourself from one organized religion to another organized religion, from one sect to another sect. Let a Hindu keep calling him or herself Hindu for the whole life. Let a Christian keep calling himself Christian for the whole life_a Muslim, Muslim; a Sikh, Sikh; a Buddhist, Buddhist. But one should become a good Hindu. One should become a good Muslim, a good Christian, a good Sikh, a good Buddhist. One should become a good human being. Dharma teaches you how to become a good human being, how to live a good life, a happy life, a harmonious life.

May all of you get trained in this wonderful technique. Come out of your misery and enjoy real peace, real harmony, real happiness. Real happiness to you all. Real happiness to you all.

*** *** ***

Questions and Answers

Q: How can we avoid karma?

A: Be the master of your own mind. The whole technique teaches you how to become your own master. If you are not the master of your mind, then because of the old habit pattern, you will keep on performing those actions, that karma, which you don't want to perform. Intellectually you understand: "I should not perform these actions." Yet you still perform them, because you do not have mastery over your mind. This technique will help you to become the master of your own mind.

Q: What is the ultimate goal of life? That is, what does all this harmony lead to?

A: The ultimate life, the ultimate goal, is here and now. If you keep looking for something in the future but you don't gain anything now, this is a delusion. If you have started experiencing peace and harmony now, then there is every likelihood that you will reach the goal, which is nothing but peace and harmony. So experience it now, at this moment. Then you are really on the right path.

Q: How can a truly Dharmic person face this adharmic world?

A: Don't try to change the adharmic world. Try to change the adharma in yourself, the way in which you are reacting and making yourself miserable. As I said, when somebody is abusing you, understand that this person is miserable. It is the problem of that person. Why make it your problem? Why start generating anger and becoming miserable? Doing that means you are not your own master, you are that person's slave; whenever that person wants to, he can make you miserable. You are the slave of someone else who is a miserable person. You have not understood Dharma. Be your own master and you can live a Dharmic life in spite of the adharmic situations all around.

Q: Is there any shorter way?

A: I would say this is the shortest way. You have to change your habit pattern; you have to go to the root of your problem. And the root of problem is inside, not outside. If you learn how to take a dip inside, if you start changing things at the root level, this is the shortest way for you to come out of your misery.

Q: Some people have impurities, but they feel happy and don't look miserable. Please explain.

A: You have not entered the minds of these people. A person may have alot of money, and others may feel: "Such a happy person. Look, he has so much wealth." But what you don't know is that this person can't get sound sleep; he has to use sleeping pills_a very miserable person. You can know for yourself how miserable you are, going deep inside. You can't understand at the external level by seeing sombody's face whether he or she is miserable or happy. The misery lies deep inside.

Q: What is the Dharma of ātma, soul?

A: Observe yourself and you will find what is happening inside. What you call "soul," what you call *ātma,* you will notice, is just a reacting mind, a certain part of the mind. Yet you remain under the illusion that: "This is 'I.' See, this is 'I,' this is 'I.'" This illusion of 'I' will go away, and then the reaction will go away, and you will be liberated from your misery. This does not happen by accepting philosophical beliefs.

Q: How to deal with insomnia?

A: Vipassana will help you. When people can't sleep properly, if they lie down and observe respiration or sensations, they can get sound sleep. Even if they don't get sound sleep, the next day they will get up feeling very fresh, as if they have come out of a deep sleep. Practise. Try, and you will find that it is very helpful.

Q: What is the relevance of Dharma to a person on the street, whose stomach is empty?

A: A large number of people living in slums come to Vipassana courses and find it very helpful. Their stomachs are empty, but theirs mind also are so agitated. With such agitated minds, they can't solve their daily problems. With Vipassana, they learn how to keep their minds calm and equanimous. Then they can face their problems. They get better results in their lives. Moreover, I have found that, although people from the slums are very poor, most of their earnings is spent on alcohol and gambling. After taking a few courses, they come out of gambling, they come out of alcohol; they come out of all kinds of addictions. Dharma is helpful. It is helpful to one and all, rich or poor. It makes no difference.

Q: What is the effect of Vipassana on the chakras of the subtle body?

A: Chakras are nothing but nerve centres on the spinal chord. Vipassana takes you to the stage where you can feel activity in every little atom of your body. Chakras are just a part of that. This activity can be experienced in the entire body.

Q: How do you define eternal life in your meditation system?

A: It is not my meditation system! It is an Indian meditation system, ancient India's meditation system. The life is eternal, but you have to make it purified, so that you live a better life, a good life. Don't try to find the beginning of life, when it started_what you will gain by that? The life is starting every moment; this ball is rolling. It is rolling in a wrong way, and you are a miserable person. Come out of that misery. That is more important than anything else.

Q: How does one escape from anger?

A: This is what Vipassana will teach you. Observe your anger, and you will come out of it. And to observe anger, you learn how to observe your respiration, and how to observe your sensations.

Q: How can professionals, who have less time, practise meditation?

A: Meditation is all the more important for professionals! Those who are householders, who have responsibilities in life, need Vipassana much more, because they have to face situations in life where there are so many vicissitudes. They become agitated because of these vicissitudes. If they learn Vipassana, they can face life much better. They can make good decisions, right decisions, correct decisions, which will be very helpful to them. For professionals, executives, and other people with responsibilities, Vipassana is a great boon.

Q: Do you believe in rebirth?

A: My believing or not believing will not help you. Meditate, and you will reach a stage where you can see your past, and you can see your future. Then only believe. Don't believe something just because your guru says so. Otherwise you will be under the clutches of a guru, which is against Dharma.

Q: What is mind? Where it is?

A: This is what you will understand by practising Vipassana. You will make an analytical study of your mind, an analytical study of your matter, and the interaction between the two.

Q: How can we make others peaceful?

A: Make yourself peaceful! Only then you can make others peaceful.

Q: I agree that this meditation will help me, but how does it solve the problems of society?

A: Society is, after all, nothing but a group of individuals. We want to solve the problems of society, yet we don't solve the problems of the individual. We want peace in the world, yet we do nothing for the peace of the individual. How is this possible? If each individual experiences peace and harmony, then we will find that the whole society starts experiencing peace and harmony.

Q: I can't suppress my anger, even if I try.

A: Don't suppress it: observe it! If you suppress it, problems will come. The more you try to suppress the anger, the more it goes to the deeper level of your mind. The complexes become stronger and stronger, and it is so difficult to come out of them. Just observe your anger. No suppression, no expression. Just observe.

Q: Are anger and observation simultaneous, or is observation a process arising after thought?

A: No, it is not a thought. You observe simultaneously, as the anger arises.

Q: If someone is purposely making our life miserable_how to tolerate this?

A: First of all, don't try to change the other person. Try to change yourself. Somebody is trying to make you miserable. But you are becoming miserable because you are reacting to this. If you learn how to observe your reaction, then nobody can make you miserable. Any amount of misery from others cannot make you miserable if you learn to remain equanimous deep inside. This technique will help you. Once you become free from misery deep inside, this will also start affecting others. The same person who was harming you will start changing little by little.

Q: Isn't excusing a sinner encouraging sin?

A: Never encourage sin. Stop people from committing sin. But don't have aversion or anger towards the sinner. Have love, have compassion. This person is a miserable person, an ignorant person, who doesn't know what he or she is doing. They are harming themselves and harming others. So you use all your strength, physical and vocal, to stop this person from committing sin, but with love and compassion towards them. This is what Vipassana will teach you.

Q: Can we get complete transformation and complete happiness through Vipassana?

A: It is a progressive process. As you start working, you will find that you are experiencing more and more happiness, and eventually you will reach the stage which is total happiness. You become more and more transformed, and you will reach the stage which is total transformation. It is progressive.

Q: What is superior to mind?

A: First know what mind is. Then you will know what is beyond mind, what is superior to mind.

Q: How do you equate religion and Dharma?

A: Well, if religion is taken as Hindu religion or Buddhist religion, and so on, then it is totally against Dharma. But if religion is taken as the law of nature, the universal law of nature, then it is the same as Dharma.

Q: How much should we practise Vipassana in our daily life?

A: Take a course, and then you will understand how to apply the practice in your life. If you just take a course and don't apply it in life, then Vipassana will become just a rite, ritual, or a religious ceremony. It won't help you. Vipassana is to live a good life. You will understand how to apply it in life after taking a course.

Q: What is depression? Is it an external, or an internal, problem?

A: All problems are internal. There are no external problems. If you go deep inside and discover the cause of your misery, you will find that every cause lies within yourself, not outside. Remove that cause, and you will be free from misery.

Q: What is the difference between Dharma and duty?

A: Whatever is helpful to you and helpful to others is your duty, is Dharma. Whatever is harmful to you and harmful to others is not your duty, because it harms you and also harms others.

Q: Suffering, war and conflict are as old as history. Do you really believe in a world of peace?

A: Well, even if a few people come out of misery, it is good. When there is darkness all around and one lamp has started giving light, it is good. And like this, if one lamp becomes ten lamps, or twenty lamps, the darkness will get dispelled here and there. There is no guarantee that the entire world will become peaceful, but as much peace as you make in yourself, that much you are helping the peace of the world.

Vipassana Meditation centre

There are 214 Vipassana meditation centres in the world out of which 95 are in India. At all these centres 10-day, short & long residential courses are held practically every month. Out of them Dhamma Giri centre is mentioned here along with Dhamma Pattana and Global Vipassana pagoda.

The addresses of these centres, their phone nos. and Schedule of courses can be had from the following website.

Website: <www.vridhamma.org>, <www.dhamma.org>

Main Centre– Dhamma Giri: Vipassana International Academy, Igatpuri, 422403, Dist. Nashik, Tel. (02553) 244076, 244086, 244144, 244440, **Website:** <www.vridhamma.org>; **Email:** <info@giri.dhamma.org>

Dhamma Pattana: Near Essel world, Gorai Creek, Borivali (W), Mumbai 400091; Tel: (022) 28452238, 33747501; **Tel-Fax:** 022-33747531, **Email:** <info@pattana.dhamma.org>; Website: <www.pattana.dhamma.org>

Global Vipassana Pagoda: Near Essel world, Gorai Creek, Borivali (W), Mumbai 400091; Tel. 022-28452235

Vipassana Research Institute: Dhamma Giri, Igatpuri.

For books, CDs & Newsletter contact:

Vipassana Research Institute
Dhamma Giri, Igatpuri 422403,
Dist. Nashik, Maharashtra
Tel: [91] (02553) 244998, 244076, 244144, 244440

(Vipassana literature published in South Indian languages can be had from local Vipassana centres)

VRI publications can be purchased ONLINE also. **Please visit:**

Website: <www.vridhamma.org>;

Email: <vri_admin@vridhamma.org>

Made in the USA
Monee, IL
07 July 2026

56548175R00048